THE LOVE ETHIC OF D. H. LAWRENCE

the love ethic of

D. H. LAWRENCE

BY MARK SPILKA

BLOOMINGTON & LONDON
INDIANA UNIVERSITY PRESS

for Jack Spilka: 1920–1952

ACKNOWLEDGMENTS

In writing about Lawrence I have received aid and encouragement from both individuals and institutions. Among the former, I am most deeply grateful to Professor David Bidney of Indiana University, whose work on myth and primitive religion has enabled me to formulate the theoretical core of the present study. I am further indebted to Professors Francis Fergusson (Rutgers University), Leslie Fiedler (Montana State University), and Harry Moore (Babson Institute), for their invaluable suggestions for the improvement of my original manuscript—suggestions made, I might add, in spite of occasional disagreement with my position, but which have always helped me to present my thoughts with greater clarity. For minor improvements of the same order I am indebted to Mr. Lawrence Janofsky of Indiana University. I would also like to express my thanks to Mrs. Frieda Lawrence Ravagli, for her kind reception of the finished manuscript, and for the generous nature of her introductory comments. Finally, I would like to thank the School of Letters and the Graduate School of Indiana University, for providing the time, opportunity, and funds for pursuing this study.

As for debts of a less personal nature, I have relied

heavily, in Chapters 5 and 6, on F. R. Leavis' excellent and definitive series on *The Rainbow* and *Women in Love* in *Scrutiny* magazine; and in Chapter 9 I have tried to amplify the position taken by Father William Tiverton, in *D. H. Lawrence and Human Existence*, on Lawrence's challenge to Christianity. A third critic, Mark Schorer, has proved helpful in his scattered articles on Lawrence; but I have been chiefly influenced by his theory of "technique as discovery," which I have tried to adopt here as a critical method.

I am also grateful to the editors of *Accent, College English, Folio, The University of Kansas City Review, Modern Fiction Studies,* and *The New Mexico Quarterly,* for permission to reprint material from this book which originally appeared in their magazines, though in somewhat different form. In addition, I would like to thank the following for permission to quote from books which they have published or control: Alfred Knopf, for material from *Assorted Articles, The Later D. H. Lawrence, The Man Who Died, The Plumed Serpent,* and *Pornography and Obscenity;* the Viking Press, for citations from *Aaron's Rod, Apocalypse, The Boy in the Bush, Fantasia of the Unconscious, Kangaroo, The Letters of D. H. Lawrence, The Lost Girl, The Lovely Lady, Phoenix, The Portable D. H. Lawrence, Psychoanalysis and the Unconscious, The Rainbow, Sea and Sardinia, Sons and Lovers, Studies in Classic American *Literature*, *Twilight in Italy*, and *Women in Love*; Random House, for quotations from *Poems by Stephen Spender*, from George Meredith's *Diana of the Crossways*, and from Samuel Butler's *The Way of All Flesh*; Dial Press, for lines from *The First Lady Chatterley*; Harper & Brothers, for an excerpt from Ernst Cassirer's *Language and Myth*; Twayne Publishers, for the essays cited from *Sex, Literature and Censorship*; New Directions, for the use of Paul Valéry's *Selected Writings* and André Gide's *Dostoievsky*; Mrs. Frieda Lawrence Ravagli, for quotations from the Florence edition of *Lady Chatterley's Lover*; Philosophical Library, for Father Tiverton's *D. H. Lawrence and Human Existence*; Charles Scribner's Sons, for *The Spirit of Mediæval Philosophy*, by Etienne Gilson; Pearn, Pollinger & Higham Ltd., for *The Trespasser* and *The White Peacock*; Chatto and Windus Ltd., for *The History of English Literature*, by Hippolyte Taine; Penguin Books Ltd., for Balzac's *Old Goriot*; and Jonathan Cape, for material from Jessie Chambers' biography, *D. H. Lawrence: A Personal Record*.

For the reader's benefit, there are supplementary notes at the end of each chapter, and a bibliography and index at the end of the book. Under ideal conditions, the notes should be read after the completion of each chapter, rather than during the initial reading.

CONTENTS

FOREWORD

*T*HIS IS a fascinating book. It tells much more than the title implies. It makes you think not only about what Lawrence believed and thought, but about his value for others. Mr. Spilka is not interested in Lawrence's personal history and his doings and wanderings, not at all. The book seems to penetrate right into the center of Lawrence's work and its meaning and speaks from there. The readers of this book will find a new Lawrence there.

Mr. Spilka writes: "But it is the inward process, the passional strife itself which claims the reader's sympathy just as the hero's verbal efforts claim his understanding." With this attitude, Mr. Spilka discovers many things, from the importance of flowers in Lawrence's writings to the special form of his novels.

The last chapters in this book are pure inspiration and triumph for Lawrence and his religious attitudes. Here is a start at revealing his significance. This book needs no introduction. It is like the launching of a ship on its course. The best of luck to its voyage.

Frieda Lawrence Ravagli

EL PRADO, NEW MEXICO, JULY 20, 1955

part one AN INTRODUCTION TO THE NOVELS

Oh, give me the novel! Let me hear what the novel says.
As for the novelist, he is usually a dribbling liar.

D. H. LAWRENCE

1.

A NOTE ON WHOLE KNOWLEDGE

For some time now it has been the custom to divide D. H. Lawrence into aesthetic and prophetic halves, one of which wrote the good portions of his novels, the other the bad. The assumption here is that Lawrence was really "secular" in his art, and prophetic only in the didactic portions of his novels—which are best forgotten. But I think it can be shown that Lawrence was a religious artist, and that all his work was governed by religious ends. In his fiction, for example, he tried to write a kind of fourth-dimensional prose, so as to give his readers the effect of religious depth. At the same time, such depth implied direction, or the movement of his language through essentially sacred realms. Now Lawrence clearly wanted to educate our feelings in these realms; he wanted to "inform and lead into new places the flow of our sympathetic consciousness"— so that his creative work seems as prophetic and didactic, in its own way, as his sermons and pronouncements.

3

Thus, to understand Lawrence properly, we need some adequate definition of his central religious impulse. Because of his belief in the life-force, he has generally been called a "vitalist." But "organicist" would come much closer to the mark, since the goal of life, for Lawrence, was organic wholeness, or the achievement of "full, spontaneous being." This is the core of his message, and interestingly enough, this is also the cause of his commitment to the novel:

I am a man, and alive [he tells us]. For this reason I am a novelist. And being a novelist, I consider myself superior to the saint, the scientist, the philosopher, and the poet, who are all great masters of different bits of man alive, but never get the whole hog. (*Phoenix,* p. 535)

In the novel, we apparently get the "whole hog," and we are able to know him in full. By reading the novel, that is,

[we] can develop an instinct for life . . . an instinct of the whole consciousness in a man, bodily, mental, spiritual at once. And only in the novel are *all* things given full play. . . . For out of the full play of all things emerges the only thing that is anything, the wholeness of a man, the wholeness of a woman, man alive, and live woman. (p. 538)

In other words, the art of the novel was *the* religious art for Lawrence. All other mediums could offer limited contact with the full play of things, and with "man alive" in the midst of them; but only in the novel could he speak to the whole man about wholeness, and speak with full authority.

In effect, this means that the best of the long and short novels stand at the peak of his achievement; they are modes of total knowledge, and only within their context can we fully understand his message. And by "understand" I mean that form of sympathetic and intellectual comprehension which any novel demands, but which Lawrence always put to an extremely formidable test. One of the chief conditions of his art, for example, was the use of instrumental intelligence on the part of his protagonist. As Lawrence explains it in *Women in Love:*

Man struggles with his unborn needs and fulfilment. New unfoldings struggle up in torment in him, as buds struggle forth from the midst of a plant. Any man of real individuality tries to know and to understand what is happening, even in himself, as he goes along. This struggle for verbal consciousness should not be left out in art. It is a very great part of life. It is not superimposition of a theory. It is the passionate struggle into conscious being. (p. x)

By "passionate struggle into conscious being," Lawrence means the emergence from some partial or mechanical state of being into organic wholeness. In most of the better fiction, the Laurentian hero undergoes this process, and his mental efforts serve, accompany, and actually help to make it possible. But it is the inward process, the passional strife itself, which claims the reader's sympathies, just as the hero's verbal efforts claim his understanding. Through these parallel yet interdependent claims, which are generated by the hero's *total* struggle, the reader gains full knowledge of "a very great part of life."

To be sure, this tends to oversimplify the problem. Other characters are grouped about the hero, and his theories have a decided effect upon their lives. On the other hand, their lives provide a decided check against his theories, so that his views *subserve* the relatedness of all things. They are purged and qualified by the pull and thrust of human interchange— and this is Lawrence's way of threshing out important problems. Thus, if the hero often looks, acts, and talks like his creator, he is only a projection of Lawrence, who stands above him and explores reality with the aid of his own image. The result is a kind of novel of discovery, didactic but experimental, prophetic but obedient to the dictates of experience. (On this count, see especially *The Later D. H. Lawrence*, ed. William York Tindall, pp. viii-ix.)

Not all of Lawrence's books will fit this definition. But most of the long and short novels are built along these lines, and a good many of them are actual triumphs in prophetic art. The present study is limited to five examples of such art: *Sons and Lovers, The Rainbow, Women in Love, Lady Chatterley's Lover,* and *The Man Who Died.* In the following chapter, I discuss the form and dimension of these novels; I try to show, for example, that Lawrence wrote about man in the universe, and that he tried to connect cosmology with psychology, or the "life-force" with a well-developed psychology of life. This pattern is amplified, in the next two chapters, as it occurs in *Sons and Lovers*. We see it there in the strange relations between men, women, and flowers, and (once the Freudian trimmings are removed) in the equally strange relations between Paul Morel and his three sweethearts. In the following chapter, on *The Rainbow*, there is an important contrast between the Laurentian scheme of things and Christian morals and metaphysics. Chapters 6 and 7 deal, respectively, with the achievement of "mystic marriage," in *Women in Love*, and of brotherhood beyond it. Then, in the closing chapters, there is the final ordering of love, both for society and the individual, as it occurs in *Lady Chatterley's Lover* and *The Man Who Died*.

In sum, these novels represent successive points of synthesis in Lawrence's development; they body forth that general pattern of experience which I would call his ethic of love—and by using the phrase "love ethic," I mean to emphasize his radical commitment to spontaneous life, and to "phallic marriage" as the fount of life itself:

From it all things human spring, children and beauty and well-made things; all the true creations of humanity.

2.

THE RELIGIOUS DIMENSION

IN HIS massive *History of English Literature,* Hippolyte Taine complains of the preoccupation with vice and virtue in the English novel, to the neglect of man's inner constitution. He concedes that moral qualities "are the finest fruit of the human plant," but holds they are not its root—"they give us our value, but do not constitute our elements," which are found instead in the realm of "primitive passions":

A character is a force [he adds], like gravity, or steam, . . . which must be defined otherwise than by the amount of weight it can lift or the havoc it can cause. It is therefore to ignore man, to reduce him . . . to an aggregate of virtues and vices; it is to lose sight in him of all but the exterior and social side; it is to neglect the inner and natural element. We will find the same fault in English criticism, always moral, never psychological, . . . we will find the same fault in English religion, which is but an emotion or a discipline; in their philosophy, destitute of metaphysics; and if we ascend to the source . . . we will see all these weaknesses derived from their native en-

8

ergy, their practical education, and that kind of severe and religious poetic instinct which has in time past made them Protestant and Puritan.

If Taine could have lived on into the present century, he would have noted, with some consternation, that the first English novelist to explore man's natural elements, and to approach them through psychology and metaphysics, was Protestant by birth and Puritan (in a restricted sense) by disposition. To make the irony more complete, this novelist trained the full force of the English moral conscience upon the realm of "primitive passions." In other words, he tried to connect the root of Taine's metaphorical plant with the fruit, and to deal as much as possible with the whole organism. But perhaps this was a better, more inclusive definition of the artist's function than the one which Taine had offered. To tell us what man is, organically, and to place value upon this, was to restore some sense of unity to the human scheme. It was this special sense of unity, then, which D. H. Lawrence brought to the English novel; indeed, he found the very goal of life in the achievement of organic being, and the only major sin—its degradation or denial.

Accordingly, he showed less interest in "vice" and "virtue," as we understand them, than in specific elements of being, such as will, sympathy, spirit, flesh, and intellect. But at the same time his interest here was moral and religious: he called for a balance of all these elements, a kind of achieved harmony which would enable men and women to live spontaneously, out of the fullness of their powers; and he deplored an imbalance of these elements, since it led towards emotional atrophy and predatory behavior. In his fiction, for example, some figures rely upon one or two elements of being, to the point where it distorts their affective life. One woman smothers a man with excessive spirituality; another tries to reduce her lover to his mental essence; or a husband tries to dominate his wife through will and sensual power. In the meantime, such figures atrophy or disintegrate from within.

The principles at odds in this psychology are those of balance and excess, wholeness and partness, sustenance and reduction. In the relations between man and woman, for instance, Lawrence called for balance or "polarity," as if between two oppositely charged entities; or he placed the marriage unit itself in balance with the world of purposive activity—so that the protagonists of his novels must also be in tune, as it were, with the world around them. In other words, they must achieve organic being through "an infinity of pure relations" with the living universe: first, with each other, through love; then with other men and women, through friendship and creative labor; and finally even with birds, beasts, and flowers, which play a vital role in all the novels.

Once this is clearly understood, his psychology begins to take on flesh and substance; it falls within a greater and essentially religious scheme of life, and draws its depth and quality from that fact. Indeed, this interpenetration of the greater universe with specific situations, of the "life-force" with a well-developed psychology of life, is the hallmark of Laurentian fiction: in *Sons and Lovers* the direct relation between men, women, and flowers sets off the inward state of each of the major characters; in *St. Mawr* Lou Witt and her husband are judged in terms of their relation to the horse, St. Mawr; and in *Women in Love,* when Gerald Crich and Gudrun Brangwen attempt to subdue the stubborn rabbit, Bismarck, they reveal themselves as decadent modern lovers, intent on destroying their own organic life, while mocking and exploiting the very flame of life, the magnificent vitality embodied by the rabbit:

"Isn't it a fool!" [cried Gudrun.] "Isn't it a sickening *fool?*" The vindictive mockery in her voice made [Gerald's] brain quiver. Glancing up at him, into his eyes, she revealed again the mocking, white-cruel recognition. There was a league between them, abhorrent to them both. They were implicated with each other in abhorrent mysteries.

"How many scratches have you?" he asked, showing his hard forearm, white and hard and torn in red gashes.

"How really vile!" she cried, flushing with a sinister vision. "Mine is nothing."

She lifted her arm and showed a deep red score down the silken white flesh.

"What a devil!" he exclaimed. But it was as if he had had knowledge of her in the long red rent of her fore-arm, so silken and soft. He did not want to touch her. He would have to make himself touch her, deliberately. The long, shallow red rip seemed torn across his own brain, tearing the surface of his ultimate consciousness, letting through the forever unconscious, unthinkable red ether of the beyond, the obscene beyond. (pp. 275-76)

This is the kind of vivid, "fourth-dimensional" prose we can expect from Lawrence at his best: and he is always at his best when revealing something about man's inner life by showing him in direct re-lation with the life around him—as in *The Man Who Died,* for a last example, with its close, vivid contact between the Christ-figure and the spunky young gamecock.

II

This special "fourth dimension" in Lawrence's work deserves much more attention than it generally re-ceives. On the one hand, there is the usual talk about the "quickness" of his prose, its spontaneity, its con-crete bulginess and surge; and on the other hand, there is the common observation that Lawrence was a religious writer. But no one thinks to put the two together, and to speak outright of the total religious dimension of his novels.[1] Granted, that Father Tiverton speaks of the sense in Lawrence's work "that what is shown as alive owes its aliveness to something behind or above—to the transcendent." But he fails to connect this observation with "dramatic" structure, and he also fails to separate Laurentian transcendence from the usual Christian sense of the term, and so deprives us of the full import of Lawrence's accomplishment.[2] But to do this problem justice, we must turn, for a moment, to an extremely pertinent theory of language, myth, and religion put forth by Ernst Cassirer. For according to Cassirer:

Language moves in the middle kingdom between the 'indefinite' and the 'infinite'; it transforms the indeterminate into a determinate idea, and then holds it within the sphere of finite determinations. So there are, in the realm of mythic and religious conception, 'ineffables' of different order, one of which represents the lower limit of verbal expression, the other the upper limit; but between these bounds, which are drawn by the very nature of verbal expression, language can move with perfect freedom, and exhibit all the wealth and concrete exemplification of its creative power. (*Language and Myth*, p. 81)

For Cassirer, then, the upper limit of language would correspond with the Christian version of the infinite, which is static, timeless, and absolute. But the "indefinite" or lower limit of language would correspond with the more primitive concept of *mana*, and presumably with any similar concept which involves a highly relative force or flow: say, Wordsworth's religious flux, Nietzsche's Dionysian force, or Bergson's *élan vital.* As for *mana* itself, Cassirer describes it as a vague, mysterious, holy power which pops up out of a mythical field of force and appears now here, now there, in any guise, in front of primitive man. That Lawrence was familiar with this concept is not difficult to prove. He utilized it in novels like *The Rainbow* and *Women in Love,* where the moon sometimes becomes a sudden "presence" to his protagonists; and he wrote about it directly in *Apocalypse,* where he deals specifically with the old Greek version of *mana,* the *theos* concept:

To the ancient consciousness . . . the universe was a great complex activity of things existing and moving and having effect. . . . Everything was *theos;* but even so, not at the same moment. At the moment, whatever *struck* you was god. If it was a pool of water, the very watery pool might strike you: then that was god; or a faint vapour at evening rising might catch the imagination: then that was *theos;* or thirst might overcome you at the sight of the water; then the thirst itself was god; or you drank, and the delicious and indescribable slaking of thirst was the god; or you felt the sudden chill of the water as you touched it: and then another god came into being, "the cold": and this was not a quality, it was an existing entity, almost a creature, certainly a *theos.* (pp. 84-85)

The difficulty which Lawrence has in describing *theos* is not his own: for primitive man, *theos* (or *mana*) was too vague and impermanent for precise description; hence he used the term as noun, verb, adjective, or adverb, with equal readiness. In fact, to describe *mana* at all, he needed an extremely fluid, volatile form of language, simply to keep pace with its manifestations, and to keep them in focus. This was the same problem, by and large, which Lawrence faced in his writing, and there is ample evidence that he actually fused the *mana* concept with his own particular view of quickness, in both life and language. We see this, unmistakably, in a passage from an essay called "The Novel":

We have to choose between the quick and the dead. The quick is God-flame, in everything. And the dead is dead. In this room where I write, there is a little table that is dead: it doesn't even weakly exist. And there is a ridiculous little iron stove, which for some unknown reason is quick. And there is an iron wardrobe trunk, which for some still more mysterious reason is quick. And there are several books, whose mere corpus is dead, utterly dead and non-existent. And there is a sleeping cat, very quick. And a glass lamp, that, alas, is dead.

What makes the difference? *Quién sabe?* But difference there is. And I *know* it.

And the sum and source of all quickness, we will call God. And the sum and total of all deadness we may call human.

And if one tries to find out, wherein the quickness of the quick lies, it is in a certain weird relationship between that which is quick and—I don't know; perhaps all the rest of things. It seems to consist in an odd sort of fluid, changing, grotesque or beautiful relatedness. That silly iron stove somehow *belongs*. Whereas this thin-shanked table doesn't belong. It is a mere disconnected lump, like a cut-off finger. And now we see the great, great merits of the novel. It can't exist without being "quick." . . . For the relatedness and interrelatedness of all things flows and changes and trembles like a stream, and like fish in the stream the characters in the novel swim and drift and float and turn belly-up when they're dead. (*The Later D. H. Lawrence,* pp. 193-94, 196)

All this is close, in a modified and intelligent way, to the *mana* concept; and we might even note, in passing, the equally close connection Lawrence makes between life and the novel, in terms of organic flow. But for the moment the points to stress are these: 1) that Lawrence had found corroboration for his independent sense of the quickness, the interrelatedness of all things, by reading the anthropologists; and 2) that he seems to have borrowed the holiness and perhaps the volatility of *mana* and merged this with his own concept of the life-flame, or with Bergson's *élan vital,* to arrive at the God-stuff—the life-force—which flows through all "live" objects and binds man to the living universe.[3] But there is even an ancient parallel for this broader view: at the primitive stage, writes Cassirer, "life possesses the same religious dignity in its humblest and in its highest forms. Men and animals, animals and plants are all on the same level" (*An Essay on Man*, p. 83). Here, then, is the "solidarity of life" principle, which brings to the Laurentian version of Nature the toughness and vitality so conspicuously missing, say, in Wordsworth's highly spiritualized form of animism. Take this lengthy excerpt from the opening pages of *The Rainbow:*

So the Brangwens came and went without fear of necessity, working hard because of the life that was in them, not for want of the money. . . . They felt the rush of the sap in spring, they knew the wave which cannot halt, but every year throws forward the seed to begetting, and, falling back, leaves the young-born on the earth. They knew the intercourse between heaven and earth, sunshine drawn into the breast and bowels, the rain sucked up in the daytime, nakedness that comes under the wind in autumn, showing the birds' nests no longer worth hiding. Their life and interrelations were such; feeling the pulse and body of the soil, that opened to their furrow for the grain, and became smooth and supple after their ploughing, and clung to their feet with a weight that pulled like desire, lying hard and unresponsive when the crops were to be shorn away. The young corn waved and was silken, and the lustre slid along the limbs of the men who saw it. They took the udder of the cows, the cows yielded milk and

pulse against the hands of the men, the pulse of the
blood of the teats of the cows beat into the pulse of the
hands of the men. They mounted their horses, and held
life between the grip of their knees, they harnessed their
horses at the wagon, and, with hand on the bridle-rings,
drew the heaving of the horses after their will. . . .

It was enough for the men, that the earth heaved and
opened its furrow to them, that the wind blew to dry the
wet wheat, and set the young ears of corn wheeling
freshly round about; it was enough that they helped the
cow in labour, or ferreted the rats from under the barn,
or broke the back of a rabbit with a sharp knock of the
hand. So much warmth and generating and pain and
death did they know in their blood, earth and sky and
beast and green plants, so much exchange and interchange they had with these, that they lived full and
surcharged, their senses full fed, their faces always
turned to the heat of the blood, staring into the sun,
dazed with looking towards the source of generation, unable to turn round. (pp. 1-3)

Lawrence is decidedly moving about, in this passage, at the lower level of language; he is dealing
with a vague but nourishing force or flow which
occurs *in time,* and which plays an important and
distinctly religious role in the novel: the Brangwen
men enjoy "blood-intimacy" with the life around
them; they must learn to utilize this contact for
creative ends; and in order to achieve organic being,
they must also learn to transcend it. But opposed to

the rainbow, or the round arch of full organic life, is the pointed arch of the cathedral, the symbol of Christianity. And to treat Christianity properly, Lawrence had to shift over to the upper level of language and deal in terms of "soul-intimacy" with the Christian infinite, during the *timeless* moment of prayer: which is precisely what happens, midway through the novel, when Will Brangwen enters Lincoln Cathedral:

Then he pushed open the door, and the great, pillared gloom was before him, in which his soul shuddered and rose from her nest. . . . His soul leapt up into the gloom, into possession, it reeled, it swooned with a great escape, it quivered in the womb, in the hush and the gloom of fecundity, like seed of procreation in ecstasy. . . .

Away from time, always outside of time! Between east and west, between dawn and sunset, the church lay like a seed in silence, dark before germination, silenced after death. Containing birth and death, potential with all the noise and transitation of life, the cathedral remained hushed, a great involved seed, whereof the flower would be radiant life inconceivable, but whose beginning and whose end were the circle of silence. Spanned round with the rainbow, the jewelled gloom folded music upon silence, light upon darkness, fecundity upon death, as a seed folds leaf upon leaf and silence upon the root and the flower, hushing up the secret of all between its parts, the death out of which it fell, the life into which it has dropped, the immortality it involves, and the death it will embrace again.

Here in the church, "before" and "after" were folded together, all was contained in oneness. . . . (p. 189)

If we compare this with the earlier passage in aim, texture and execution, we can see at once how Lawrence worked at opposite levels of language, and with two distinct concepts of the ineffable. That he could do so successfully is not simply an indication of his versatility, but a confirmation of the actual religious dimension of his writings.[4] We find this same striking contrast, for example, in other works: in *Sons and Lovers* there is the close, heavy, timeless spiritual communion over flowers between Paul Morel and Miriam Leivers, and there is the bright, open, sensual engagement with the natural world which Paul and his mother enjoy; in *The Man Who Died* there is the dramatic contrast between the cold timeless nullity of the tomb and the bloom of life in the peasant's yard:

The man who had died looked nakedly on life, and saw a vast resoluteness everywhere flinging itself up in stormy or subtle wave-crests, foam-tips emerging out of the blue invisible, a black and orange cock or the green flame-tongues out of the extremes of the fig-tree. They came forth, these things and creatures of spring, glowing with desire and with assertion. They came like crests of foam, out of the blue flood of the invisible desire, out of the vast invisible sea of strength, and they came coloured and tangible, evanescent, yet deathless in their coming. (pp. 19-20)

Even the young gamecock is a crest on "the swaying ocean of life," and we see, perhaps for the first time, that the quickness and spontaneity of Lawrence's prose—its transcendent quality—is almost always "supplied" by the primitive indefinite, the life-force, and not by the Christian infinite.

Thus Lawrence singles out "the sensual passions and mysteries" in his foreword to *Women in Love;* he calls them "equally sacred with the spiritual mysteries and passions," and finds that "the only thing unbearable is the degradation, the prostitution of the living mysteries in us." And by "living mysteries" Lawrence means those vague emotional aspects of human experience which coincide, he feels, with the primitive indefinite. Hence this rolling evocation of love, as pure inward experience, from *The First Lady Chatterley:*

Suddenly, in the deeps of her body wonderful rippling thrills broke out where before there had been nothingness; and rousing strange, like peals of bells ringing themselves in her body, more and more rapturously, the new clamour filled her up, and she heard and did not hear her own short wild cries as the rolling of the magnificent thrills grew more and more tremendous, then suddenly started to ebb away in a richness like the after humming of great bells.

And then she lay lapped in a new womb, a new throbbing of life all round her. And she loved the man, loved him with all the depths of her body and her body's splendid soul. . . . And suddenly she clung to his body again in the last surge of gratitude that lifted her as on a wave to him. (p. 63)

The "wave" here is the greater wave of life, and the act of love involves the nourishing, sacred flow of life between man and woman: that is what Lawrence believed, that love is a religious experience, a communion of the blood which brings renewed vitality of being as well as children, and which serves to confirm our close involvement with the living universe.[5]

But in contrast to all this, "counterfeit love" proves destructive and exhaustive; it stems, says Lawrence, from purely mental feelings, from "white, cold, nervous, 'poetic,' personal" desire, which exhausts the "life-flow" with its frictional insistence. So the chief moral criterion for love in Lawrence's world, or for *any* emotional experience, is this: does it affirm or deny, renew or destroy, the sacred life within us? For it must be made emphatically clear that Lawrence saw all human engagements, sexual or otherwise, in terms of their effect upon the soul's vitality. But when even a simple conversation leaves us feeling debased, or an awkward interview proves humiliating, then plainly our own experience tends to confirm, at the least, the general lines of his theory.[6]

Lawrence was not an incredible mystic; his grasp of human exchange was impressively sound; his sense of the quick and the dead, uniquely strong. Indeed, the resurrection or destruction of the human soul, within the living body, was the major theme of all his work; and by resurrection Lawrence meant no more, and in all fairness no less, than emergence into greater fullness of being: hence the struggle to transcend mere "blood-intimacy" with the life-force in *The Rainbow;* or the struggle to regain that lost vitality in *Lady Chatterley's Lover,* after the long trek around the world had convinced Lawrence of the general sterility of modern life. So he had often preached the need to waken the phallic or bodily forms of consciousness in man; but more than this, he had always preached the "Holy Ghost" life, or the life of the self in its wholeness: "the individual in his pure singleness, in his totality of consciousness, in his oneness of being: the Holy Ghost which is with us after our Pentecost, and which we may not deny" (*Fantasia of the Unconscious,* p. 191).

The resurrection, then, is to greater fullness of being, and with this in mind, we can begin to understand the curious ritual pattern of Lawrence's work: those daily rites with the sun, for example, in the strange short story, *Sun;* or the pledge to life-destruction in the rabbit scene from *Women in Love;* or the floral rites in *Sons and Lovers,* where the living relationship between men, women and flowers is used to push the story along: and for this, take Mrs. Morel's garden-swoon, before Paul's birth; or the whole attempt by Paul and Miriam to commune over flowers, *a la Wordsworth;* or the extraordinary flower-picking scene between Paul, Miriam, and Clara; the floral benediction as Paul and Clara make love; and finally, the spontaneous gift of flowers to Miriam as the novel ends. But this is not the place for any thorough explication. For the moment, I simply want to emphasize that most of Lawrence's works move forward through ritual scenes, toward ritualistic ends. For just as the essence of religious ritual is communion, so Lawrence saw all deeply significant contacts—between human beings, or even between man and the living universe—as spontaneous forms of communion, either sacred or debased, either nourishing or reductive; and just as the old primitive "rites of passage" always center around such basic events as birth, rebirth into manhood, death, and resurrection to the greater life beyond, so Lawrence's stories always center around rebirth and death—the emergence into greater or lesser forms of being. But if this is true, then the sexual scenes in *Lady Chatterley's Lover* can only be understood as "dramatic" rites of communion. And even the famous moon scenes, in both *Women in Love* and *The Rainbow,* can only be understood in terms of actual rapport, pro and con, between the protagonists and the moon-as-living-force: these men and women participate, that is to say, in ritualistic situations which fall within the larger flow of the novels. And so, as the novels move along, these figures rise up toward organic being as certain statues by Rodin rise up out of a raw rough marble base—still rooted in the vague unknown, but nonetheless organic in themselves.

III

The pattern suggested here is a complicated one, but a typical short story, "The Blind Man," may help to clarify its basic elements. The central characters of the story are Maurice Pervin, who comes home blind and badly disfigured from World War I; his wife Isabel, a woman with intellectual tastes who luxuriates, nonetheless, in passionate love; and Bertie Reid, her second or third cousin, a sort of intellectual neuter with whom she once enjoyed some cultural rapport. Bertie's visit to the Pervin farm, after a long absence, gives the story its impetus, but the emotional context of that visit deserves some attention here.

In the year since Maurice's return, the Pervins have enjoyed complete and deeply satisfying love; they have isolated themselves from society and have built a rich, dark world together, in keeping with Maurice's blindness: he tends to menial tasks about the farm, she reviews books for a Scottish newspaper, and they talk, sing, and read together "in a wonderful and unspeakable intimacy." Pervin himself has always been a sensual man, but now, feeling his way about the farm, drenched always in darkness, his whole sensual apparatus is aroused and transformed, as it were, into a new center of consciousness.

Pervin moved about almost unconsciously in his familiar surroundings, dark though everything was. He seemed to know the presence of objects before he touched them. It was a pleasure to him to rock thus through a world of things, carried on the flood in a sort of blood-prescience. He did not think much or trouble much. So long as he kept this sheer immediacy of blood-contact with the substantial world he was happy, he wanted no intervention of visual consciousness. In this state there was a certain rich positivity, bordering sometimes on rapture. Life seemed to move in him like a tide lapping, lapping and advancing, enveloping all things darkly. It was a pleasure to stretch forth the hand and meet the unseen object, clasp it, and possess it in pure contact. He did not try to remember, to visualize. He did not want to. The new way of consciousness substituted itself in him. (*The Portable D. H. Lawrence*, pp. 91-92)

This new way of consciousness is the famous "phallic" or bodily form of consciousness, and Pervin's sense of the life-flow can easily be traced to its awakening. His blindness has resulted, then, in a change of being, and this change has led in turn to closer contact with the "primitive indefinite." This is the nature of his emotional state, and a moment later Lawrence reveals its direction:

The rich suffusion of this state generally kept him happy, reaching its culmination in the consuming passion for his wife. But at times the flow would seem to be checked and thrown back. Then it would beat inside him like a tangled sea, and he was tortured in the shattered chaos of his own blood. He grew to dread this arrest, this throw-back, this chaos inside himself, when he seemed merely at the mercy of his own powerful and conflicting elements. How to get some measure of control or surety, this was the question. And when the question rose maddening in him, he would clench his fists as if he would *compel* the whole universe to submit to him. But it was in vain. He could not even compel himself.

So Pervin, like the Brangwen men in *The Rainbow,* is caught and held within a state of blood-prescience. And the potential danger of that state is kept in focus by a series of ritual scenes. The blind man moves forward toward his wife, Isabel, for example, out of the fecund darkness of the barn. His wife can actually *feel* him coming toward her, and the darkness itself seems like "a strange swirl of violent life . . . upon her." She feels giddy, and afraid even of her husband as she meets him in his own rich world of unresolved blood-intimacy. So that the scene can only be described, in ritualistic terms, as a communion of fear.

Then Bertie Reid arrives at the farm, and a second dramatic scene occurs as husband and wife take dinner with their special guest. And here, in the safety of the house, the scar on Pervin's face suggests some form of limitation or arrest to Isabel. The scar strikes Bertie this way too. He looks away from it with difficulty, and, "without knowing what he [does]," he picks up "a little crystal bowl of violets" and sniffs at them. The flowers, of course, are alive and organic, while Pervin remains fixed within a single form of consciousness. Thus an awkward moment occurs when Reid places them in Maurice's hands, so that he may smell them too. Both Isabel and Reid are afraid and deeply disturbed at this point, and again we have, in ritualistic terms, a mounting communion of fear.

This fear is dissolved, however, with the final ritual scene. Later that evening, Bertie looks for Maurice and finds him in the barn, pulping turnips. The two begin to chat about Isabel's happiness, Maurice's scar, and the casual nature of their own acquaintanceship. Then Maurice suddenly asks if he may touch him. Bertie complies, reluctantly, and Maurice gathers his head in his sensitive fingers, shifts and adjusts his grasp until he has covered the whole face, then grasps the shoulder, arm and hand before him. The bachelor lawyer feels annihilated by all this; he quivers with revulsion as Maurice asks him now to touch his own blind eyes. But again he complies.

He lifted his hand, and laid the fingers on the scar, on the scarred eyes. Maurice suddenly covered them with his own hand, pressed the fingers of the other man upon his disfigured eye-sockets, trembling in every fibre, and rocking slightly, slowly, from side to side. He remained thus for a minute or more, whilst Bertie stood as if in a swoon, unconscious, imprisoned.

Then suddenly Maurice removed the hand of the other man from his brow, and stood holding it in his own.

"Oh, my God," he said, "we shall know each other now, shan't we? We shall know each other now." (p. 103)

A writer like James Joyce might see an "epiphany" in such an experience—a static, timeless manifestation of some spiritual essence; but Lawrence sees instead a kinetic transformation of being, in both Pervin and Reid: for when the two return to Isabel, Maurice stands "with his feet apart, like a strange colossus," while Bertie is now "like a mollusc whose shell is broken." Through the friendship rite, one man moves toward greater fullness of being; his blindness is transcended, his unresolved blood-intimacy released, and the limited circle of marriage itself is broken by "the new delicate fulfillment of mortal friendship"; but the other man is destroyed by the experience; his outer bulwark against life is smashed, his inner vacuum thoroughly exposed. Thus the ritual pattern of the story is complete.

This general pattern, this ritualistic movement toward organic being, would seem to vitiate the

usual charges against Lawrence: that he had no operative sense of form; that his work was merely im-
pressionistic; or that he kept remarkable faith with
the living moment, yet never produced a complete
work of art.[7] As Frederick Hoffman states it:

Form for Lawrence was unimportant—though he was
capable of writing aptly finished short tales and novel-
ettes, his longer novels are held together by a succession
of moments of crucial experience; its continuity is fitful,
the *modus vivendi* a series of revitalized crises of bodily
relationship. (*Freudianism and the Literary Mind,* p.
177)

This criticism is sound, in part, but Hoffman
falsely assumes that emotional life is formless in itself. Lawrence apparently felt otherwise. His faith
in the living moment was uniquely counterbalanced
by his faith in the human soul, whose death and
resurrection, within the living body, was his chief
concern. And so, to accommodate his concept of the
soul, as a stable but ever-changing element, a kind
of second ego which moves along within the flux of
life, waxing and waning in accord with man's emotional experience, he discovered and employed emotional form; he learned to deal directly and obliquely
with specific states of being: in other words, he
learned to chronicle the movements of the soul. Thus,
in the better part of his works, the "crucial moments"
always mount or flow toward definite ends, and Hoff-

man, among others, fails to account for this fact. Granted, the emotional form breaks down or backs against itself, like Pervin's sensual flow, whenever Lawrence wrestles with those problems which he cannot solve. But significantly enough, this break-down coincides with the troubled middle period of his life—the period stretching from *The Lost Girl* through *Aaron's Rod, Kangaroo, The Boy in the Bush,* and *The Plumed Serpent.* But the four major novels—those which express his finest psychological and moral insights—are all well-organized along ritualistic lines. It seems scarcely accidental, then, that a man is born at the end of *Sons and Lovers;* a woman, as *The Rainbow* ends; while in *Women in Love* a man and a woman meet and marry—and con-ceive a child some eight years later, in *Lady Chat-terley's Lover.* For these four novels represent an impressive and decidedly artistic attempt, on Law-rence's part, to set forth the conditions of manhood, womanhood, and marriage, as he felt or understood them in his own life. These novels coincide, that is, with his own "rites of passage"—with the early years of elopement and self-discovery, and with the later years of maturity, when he was able to synthesize his material and to give new order to the experience of love.

NOTES

1. No one, that is to say, except Lawrence himself, who asks the rhetorical question:

> In every great novel, who is the hero all the time? Not any of the characters, but some unnamed and nameless flame behind them all. . . . In the great novel, the felt but unknown flame stands behind all the characters, and in their words and gestures there is a flicker of the presence. (*The Later D. H. Lawrence,* p. 193)

He also finds a fourth-dimensional quality in all "true and vivid relationships," and calls the novel "the highest example of subtle inter-relatedness that man has discovered." For the best expositions of this theory, see "The Novel," in *Reflections on the Death of a Porcupine* (or in *The Later D. H. Lawrence*), and "Morality and the Novel," in *Phoenix.*

2. In spite of these shortcomings, Father Tiverton moves us very far in the right direction in *D. H. Lawrence and Human Existence.* Here, for example, is an illuminating passage on Lawrence's gift for expressing "states of being hitherto . . . unexpressed":

> It is in the relatedness of the self with the other-self, and of the self with the sub-self—trees, horses, snakes, rocks, seed and flower—that the human unconscious can meet the conscious mind and so the self become aware of the self. And when this happens, the gods are pricking nature into life. As one reads Lawrence's descriptions one is suddenly aware that he is not merely describing: he is pushing an electric current through the bit of the world that stands before him, and immediately that world falls apart into two—one half of it suddenly becomes erect, shudders and

bristles with life; the other half burns in a flash and shrivels into dead grey ash. (p. 127)

3. To establish Lawrence's "independent sense" of related-ness, we need only compare this passage from *The Tres-passer* (1912) with the "God-flame" passage from "The Novel" (1925):

> The furniture, excepting the piano, had a transitory look. . . . The only objects of sympathy in the room were the white lamp that glowed on a stand near the wall, and the large, beautiful fern, with narrow fronds, which ruffled its cloud of green within the gloom of the window-bay. These only, with the fire, seemed friendly. (pp. 2-3)

As for Bergson's supposed influence on Lawrence, there is evidence that Lawrence read him for the first time in April 1913. But even before that he had written independently of the "life-flame" in *Sons and Lovers* and in a letter to Ernest Collings (January 1913):

> I conceive a man's body as a kind of flame, like a candle flame, forever upright and yet flowing: and the intellect is just the light shed on the things around. And I am not so much concerned with the things around—which is really mind—but with the mystery of the flame forever flowing, coming God knows how from out of practically nowhere, and being *itself*, whatever there is around it, that it lights up. (*Letters*, p. 96)

4. There is a standing quarrel as to whether a writer can actually evoke the ineffable, or as Cassirer would have it, the *ineffables*, the mythic or primitive indefinite and the religious infinite. In the present book, I am simply contending that when a writer consciously and effectively creates the sense of an extra dimension in his work, then that work has four dimensions. This is as true of Fielding's novels, where Provi-

dence is always "dramatically" at work, as it is of *symboliste* poetry or *The Divine Comedy* or Wordsworth's animistic poems; but whether it is true of life is a large question. Cassirer seems to think it is; Lawrence obviously felt that it was, and he tried to evoke the primitive indefinite in most of his books and poems.

5. In addition to sexual communion, there is a second major approach to the primitive indefinite, in Lawrence's world, through "passionate, purposive activity." Such activity is selfless and spiritual, and though it corresponds to Christian prayer in these respects, it occurs *in time,* and within the context of ordinary experience; besides this, it is "passionate" or vaguely emotional activity, so that it falls *below* the level of exact verbal definition, whereas the Christian consummation with the infinite occurs *above* this level, outside of time, and outside the realm of ordinary experience. For further discussion of the problem, see Chapters 5 and 9.

6. The work of other novelists also tends to confirm the general lines of Lawrence's theory. Thus Balzac writes that "feeling affects everything, and can cross space" (*Père Goriot,* p. 138) or Conrad deals with characters like Jim, in *The Nigger of the Narcissus,* and Charles Gould, in *Nostromo,* who sap the vitality of those who love them; and in *The Way of All Flesh,* Samuel Butler presents a definition of "crossing," or regeneration, which comes quite close to the Laurentian notion of communion:

> Seeing is a mode of touching, touching is a mode of feeding, feeding is a mode of assimilation, assimilation is a mode of re-creation and reproduction, and this is crossing —shaking yourself into something else and something else into you. (p. 353)

7. In *The Twentieth Century Novel,* Joseph Warren Beach holds that Lawrence was not concerned with the dramatic

shape of a thing, but with the living feel of it, and that he really painted "shimmering protoplasm," in emulation of the impressionists: "It is this shimmeriness which is the chief contribution of Lawrence to novelistic technique. . . . He is, in the novel, very little of the dramatist and very much of the poet" (p. 384). Francis Fergusson's approach, that Lawrence is chiefly valuable for his amazing sensibility, tends to support this argument (*Forms of Modern Fiction*, ed. W. V. O'Connor). But a little known article by Max Wildi comes much closer to the truth. Wildi calls Lawrence an *expressionist;* he cites his ability to express essential states of being, and calls attention to an important dramatic fact about Lawrence's characters:

> The situations that Lawrence imagines for them are symbolical, like the situations of a morality-play, and show the passage of the soul from the Flux of Corruption, the Reduction to Sensation . . . to Rebirth or Annihilation. (*English Studies*, December 1937)

Had Mr. Wildi said "ritualistic" instead of "symbolical," he would have hit upon the real movement of Lawrence's work. This is precisely how Mark Schorer handles the problem, for example, in the *Kenyon Review*, Winter 1952:

> More and more he managed fiction in which the action itself was ritualistic and the prose liturgical, until in the end he wrote nearly pure symbolic dramas like *The Plumed Serpent* and *Lady Chatterley's Lover*, or directly in the forms of fable, as in *The Woman Who Rode Away* and *The Man Who Died*.

This is a good historical description, but it fails to account for the "emotional form" in earlier novels, or for the religious dimension which I deal with in this chapter. Similarly, Frank Amon correctly labels Lawrence's *rites de passage* as transitions "into another sphere of being"; but in his actual handling of the fiction he is chiefly concerned with *symbolical* patterns, and shows no genuine grasp of "emotional form" (*The Achievement of D. H. Lawrence,* ed. F. J. Hoffman and H. T. Moore).

part two   SONS AND LOVERS

She put a sucker into one's soul, and sucked up one's essential life. . . . I *know* I've got a heart. . . . But it's almost sucked dry.

FROM "THE LOVELY LADY"

3.

HOW TO PICK FLOWERS

FATHER TIVERTON has observed, quite shrewdly, that Lawrence had to die as a son before he could become a great artist. That death is chronicled, he thinks, at the end of *Sons and Lovers,* as Paul Morel refuses to follow his mother towards the grave:

> But no, he would not give in. Turning sharply, he walked towards the city's gold phosphorescence. His fists were shut, his mouth set fast. He would not take that direction, to the darkness, to follow her. He walked towards the faintly humming, glowing town, quickly. (p. 491)

Paul's death as a son implies his birth here as a man, and the potential birth of Lawrence himself as man and artist. It is a tenable theory, and from a biographical point of view, an important one.

But there are a number of other ways, equally important, in which *Sons and Lovers* serves as the matrix for all of Lawrence's future work. The structural rhythms of the book are based, for example, upon poetic rather than narrative logic: the language backs and fills with the struggle between Walter and Gertrude Morel; in the scenes between Paul and Miriam Leivers, the tempo is labored and strained; then it quickens perceptibly when Paul is with Clara Dawes. In each case, the emotional predicament determines the pace of the language, so that the novel surges along, always in key with the inward tensions of the protagonists: and this will prove the general rule in future novels.[1]

But Lawrence makes a more crucial connection in this book between language and emotion: for the symbolic scenes are extremely literal, and the symbols seem to function as integral strands in the web of emotional tensions. They are seldom used in the Elizabethan sense, as mere omens of supernatural pleasure or displeasure; instead they seem to express some close relationship between man and nature. Thus Mrs. Morel holds her unwanted baby, Paul, up to the sun, the literal source of life, in a gesture of renunciation; and Morel himself stands fascinated, after a violent quarrel with his wife, as the drops of her blood soak into their baby's scalp—and this literal sealing of the blood-tie breaks his manhood; later on, the young lad Paul stares fixedly at the blood-red moon, which has roused in him his first violent sexual passion—and roused it as a force, not as a symbol. In each case, the relation between man and nature is direct and vital, and sun, blood, and moon are more "integral" than symbolic. This too will prove the general rule in future novels, though no one seems to have recognized, as yet, this rather overwhelming truth about Lawrence's use of symbols.[2]

In *The Later D. H. Lawrence*, for example, Professor William Tindall treats Lawrence as a symbolist, and he tries to align him with the *correspondance* tradition established by Baudelaire. But the French symbolists were searching for the spiritual infinite, and Lawrence was not: his symbols operate at a different level of language than theirs, and for different ends; they are not suggestive evocations of timeless spiritual reality, but material and focal expressions of those vague but powerful forces of nature which occur, quite patently, in time.[3] In the short story "Sun," for example, a woman moves from the sterile touch of her husband to life-giving contact with the sun.

It was not just taking sun-baths. It was much more than that. Something deep inside her unfolded and relaxed, and she was given. By some mysterious power inside her, deeper than her known consciousness and will, she was put into connection with the sun, and the stream flowed of itself, from her womb. She herself, her conscious self, was secondary, a secondary person, almost an onlooker. The true Juliet was this dark flow from her deep body to the sun. (*The Later D. H. Lawrence*, p. 348)

A symbolical flow? No, not even a face-saving *correspondance*. Lawrence means what he says here, though embarrassed critics like Tindall will always blithely cancel out his meaning: "the heroine in *Sun,*" he writes, "responds with her little blazing consciousness to the 'great blazing consciousness' of heaven. There she lies naked, laughing to herself, with a flower in her navel. Her behavior may seem odd—but only when the symbolic receives a literal interpretation" (p. xv). But there is no other interpretation. The story stands or falls on the woman's living contact with the sun. The connection is organic and dramatic, and what Tindall really finds odd here is the thought that man can live in anything but an alien universe.

Most modern readers will side with Tindall in this respect, but Lawrence felt otherwise, and the only point I want to make is this: that he always wrote otherwise—as if the sun were not merely a gas ball but a source of life, and the moon not merely a satellite but a living force.

II

Strangely enough, he first began to write this way in *Sons and Lovers,* his third and supposedly his most conventional novel. It seems ironic, then, that Mark Schorer should criticise him for failing to use "technique as discovery" in this book—especially when he actually employs here his most characteristic techniques to discover things which Mr. Schorer over-looks, or perhaps ignores, in his justly famous essay.[4] For Lawrence makes his first ambitious attempt, in *Sons and Lovers*, to place his major characters in active relation with a live and responsive universe: and this helps to account, I think, for the strange subjective power of the novel.

We get only a slight hint of this arrangement in the case of Walter Morel. As the book develops, he gradually breaks his own manhood; but this breakdown coincides with an actual shrinkage in physique, and this shrinkage seems to come from the direct contact between Morel and the forces of nature. Thus, instead of facing his problems at home, Morel loves to slip off with his friends for good times; on one of these drunken sprees he falls asleep in an open field, and then wakens, an hour later, feeling queer—and the physical breakdown begins here, with Morel in the act of denying his own manhood. During the bout of illness which follows, his wife begins to cast him off, and she turns to the children, for the first time, "for love and life." Admittedly, the incident is more illusive than real, but the natural contact is there, and it becomes more clearly evident at other points in the novel, when the forces of nature emerge as actual "presences." Before Paul's birth, for example, the drunken Morel shuts his wife out into the garden, and she feels these presences under the "blinding" August moon:

She became aware of something about her. With an effort she roused herself to see what it was that penetrated her consciousness. The tall white lilies were reel-
ing in the moonlight, and the air was charged with their
perfume, as with a presence. Mrs. Morel gasped slightly
in fear. She touched the big, pallid flowers on their
petals, then shivered. They seemed to be stretching in
the moonlight. She put her hand into one white bin: the
gold scarcely showed on her fingers by moonlight. She
bent down to look at the binful of yellow pollen; but it
only appeared dusky. Then she drank a deep draught
of the scent. It almost made her dizzy. (pp. 30-31)

Conscious only of the child within her, Mrs. Morel
feels herself melting away: "After a time the child,
too, melted with her in the mixing-pot of moonlight,
and she rested with the hills and lilies and houses, all
swum together in a kind of swoon." Later, when
Morel lets her back into the house, she smiles faintly
upon seeing her face in the bedroom mirror, "all
smeared with the yellow dust of lilies." Both mother
and unborn child have been enveloped by the powerful dark forces of life (they have not merged with
the "infinite"), and the dust becomes a kiss of benediction for them both, the confirmation of their vitality. Later on, in *Aaron's Rod*, Lawrence would see
the same flower, the lily, as a symbol of vital individuality—"Flowers with good roots in the mud and
muck . . . fearless blossoms in air"—and Lilly, the

Lawrence-figure in the book, would personify this vitality and aloofness in name and deed.[5]

As these thoughts indicate, flowers are the most important of the "vital forces" in *Sons and Lovers*. The novel is saturated with their presence, and Paul and his three sweethearts are judged, again and again, by their attitude toward them, or more accurately, by their *relations* with them. The "lad-and-girl" affair between Paul and Miriam, for example, is a virtual communion between the two lovers and the flowers they both admire. And this communion begins with Paul's first words to the shy, romantic girl, on their meeting at Willey Farm:

He was in the garden smelling the gillivers and looking at the plants, when the girl came out quickly to the heap of coal which stood by the fence.

"I suppose these are cabbage-roses?" he said to her, pointing to the bushes along the fence. . . .

"I don't know," she faltered. "They're white with pink middles."

"Then they're maiden-blush."

Miriam flushed. . . . (pp. 149-50)

As the book moves on, the identification of Miriam with maiden-blush is broadened to imply an unhealthy spirituality. Paul grows to hate her worshipful, fawning attitude toward life, an attitude which is consistently revealed by her "relations" with flowers: "When she bent and breathed a flower, it was

as if she and the flower were loving each other. Paul
hated her for it. There seemed a sort of exposure
about the action, something too intimate" (p. 205).
This hatred bursts into open resentment as their
affair draws toward an end. One day Paul lashes out
at the girl, at Willey Farm, for caressing daffodils:

> Can you never like things without clutching them as
> if you wanted to pull the heart out of them? . . .
> You wheedle the soul out of things. . . . I would never
> wheedle—at any rate, I'd go straight. . . .
> You're always begging things to love you . . . as if you
> were a beggar for love. Even the flowers, you have to
> fawn on them . . . (p. 257)

In another context, Lawrence attacks Wordsworth himself for a similar offense—for attempting
to melt down a poor primrose "into a Williamish
oneness":

> He didn't leave it with a soul of its own. It had to have
> his soul. And nature had to be sweet and pure, William-
> ish. Sweet-Williamish at that! Anthropomorphized! An-
> thropomorphism, that allows nothing to call its soul its
> own, save anthropos. . . . (*The Later D. H. Lawrence,*
> p. 209)

But the primrose was alive in its own right, for
Lawrence; it had "its own peculiar primrosy identity
. . . its own individuality." And once again his approach to nature is primitive and direct, an affirma-
tion of the "religious dignity" of life "in its humblest

and in its highest forms." For if men, animals and plants are all on the same level, at the primitive stage, then none of them can readily usurp the other's souls.

We can safely say, then, that Miriam is Wordsworth, at least in her attitude toward nature, or toward flowers. She is finally damned by Paul as a nun, and certainly this recalls those famous lines by Wordsworth: "It is a beauteous evening, calm and free; /The holy time is quiet as a nun/ Breathless with adoration. . . ." Of course, the metaphor is appropriate within context, but Lawrence would never reduce nature to the bloodless spirituality of a nun, with no vitality of its own.

Yet in the early stages of *Sons and Lovers,* Paul Morel, the Lawrence-figure, has actually joined with Miriam in such bloodless communions over flowers. He has even taken pride in bringing them to life in the girl's imagination, and their love has its beginning "in this atmosphere of subtle intimacy, this meeting in their common feeling for something in nature. . . ." But as we know, Miriam's approach to nature is ultimately deadly, and this is the key to the dissembling of their love: she loves Paul as she loves flowers, she worships him as she worships them, and Paul feels suffocated by such adoration. This feeling is heavily underscored, for example, in the early "lad-and-girl" courtship scenes: one evening, as the two of them walk through the woods, Miriam leads

Paul on, eagerly, to a wild-rose bush she has previously discovered.

They were going to have a communion together—something that thrilled her, something holy. He was walking beside her in silence. They were very near to each other. She trembled, and he listened, vaguely anxious. . . . Then she saw her bush.

"Ah!" she cried, hastening forward.

It was very still. The tree was tall and straggling. It had thrown its briers over a hawthorn-bush, and its long streamers trailed thick, right down to the grass, splashing the darkness everywhere with great spilt stars, pure white. In bosses of ivory and in large splashed stars the roses gleamed on the darkness of foliage and stems and grass. Paul and Miriam stood close together, silent, and watched. Point after point the steady roses shone out to them, seeming to kindle something in their souls. The dusk came like smoke around, and still did not put out the roses.

Paul looked into Miriam's eyes. She was pale and expectant with wonder, her lips were parted, and her dark eyes lay open to him. His look seemed to travel down into her. Her soul quivered. It was the communion she wanted. . . . (pp. 189-90)

But once the communion "takes," once Paul has brought the roses into her soul (for their anthropomorphic slaughter), he turns aside, feeling pained, anxious, and imprisoned. They part quickly, and he stumbles away toward home—"as soon as he was out of the wood, in the free open meadow, where he could breathe, he started to run as fast as he could. It was like a delicious delirium in his veins."

A few pages later, Lawrence describes a similar scene between Paul and his mother, and the contrast is brilliantly revealing. Mrs. Morel has just discovered three deep blue scyllas under a bush in the garden. She calls Paul to her side excitedly:

"Now just see those! . . . I was looking at the currant-bushes, when, thinks I to myself, 'There's something very blue; is it a bit of sugar-bag?' and there, behold you! Sugar-bag! Three glories of the snow, and such beauties! But where on earth did they come from?"

"I don't know. . . ."

"Well, that's a marvel, now! I *thought* I knew every weed and blade in this garden. But *haven't* they done well? You see, that gooseberry-bush just shelters them. Not nipped, not touched! . . ."

"They're a glorious color! . . ."

"Aren't they! . . . I guess they come from Switzerland, where they say they have such lovely things. Fancy them against the snow! . . ."

She was full of excitement and elation. The garden was an endless joy to her. . . . Every morning after breakfast she went out and was happy pottering about in it. And it was true, she knew every weed and blade. (pp. 194-95)

The vitality, the animation, the healthy glow of the life-flame, is typical of Mrs. Morel. Always, when

Paul brings her flowers, the scene is gay, lively, warm, or poignant. If the cold family parlor "kills every bit of a plant you put in [it]," outside, in the garden or in the open fields, mother and son are always in bright and vital contact with the nodding heads of surrounding flowers.

But the most powerful of the floral scenes takes place between Paul and his rival sweethearts, Miriam Leivers and Clara Dawes. And here Richard Aldington makes a terrible (and perhaps typical) blunder, in his *Portrait of a Genius But . . .* : he attempts to show Lawrence's willfulness and inconsistency (his *but-ness*) by referring to the way Paul and Miriam (*i.e.*, Lawrence and Jessie Chambers) touch flowers: "what was wrong for her was right for him if he happened to want to do it." [6] But this is to miss the whole beauty of the most important revelation scene in *Sons and Lovers,* the scene in which Paul, Miriam, and Clara are together on Lawrence's favorite battleground: an open field in the country. Paul and Clara have just been formally introduced; he is passionately attracted to her, and eventually he will become her lover. But Miriam is aware of this attraction, and she has actually arranged the whole meeting as a test; for she believes that her hold on Paul's "higher" nature, his soul, will prevail over his desires for "lower" things—Clara's body. And her belief seems to be borne out when the three of them come to an open field, with its many "clusters of strong flowers." Ah! cries Miriam, and her eyes meet Paul's. They commune. Clara sulks. Then Paul and Miriam begin to pick flowers:

He kneeled on one knee, quickly gathering the best blossoms, moving from tuft to tuft restlessly, talking softly all the time. Miriam plucked the flowers lovingly, lingering over them. He always seemed to her too quick and almost scientific. Yet his bunches had a natural beauty more than hers. He loved them, but as if they were his and he had a right to them. She had more reverence for them: they held something she had not. (p. 279)

And there is the crux of the matter: the flowers hold life as Paul himself holds life: his contact with the "God-stuff" is spontaneous and direct—he is alive and organic, and the flowers are his to take. But negative, spiritual, sacrificial Miriam "wheedle[s] the soul out of things"; she kills life and has no right to it. What is wrong for her is actually right for him, since life kindles life and death kills it— which is the essence of Laurentian communion.

But the revelation process now extends to Clara Dawes. She has already been sketched out as a disconsolate suffragette, and now she states, militantly, that flowers shouldn't be picked because it kills them. What she means, in effect, is that *she* doesn't want to be "picked" or taken by any man; she has separated from her husband, and for her the flowers become as proud and frigid, in their isolation, as she would like to be in hers. But since Paul believes that life belongs to the living, he begins to argue the point with her; then, as the scene unfolds, he shifts from rational argument to pagan flower dance:

Clara's hat lay on the grass not far off. She was kneeling, bending forward still to smell the flowers. Her neck gave him a sharp pang, such a beautiful thing, yet not proud of itself just now. Her breasts swung slightly in her blouse. The arching curve of her back was beautiful and strong; she wore no stays. Suddenly, without knowing, he was scattering a handful of cowslips over her hair and neck, saying:

"Ashes to ashes, and dust to dust,
If the Lord won't have you the devil must."

The chill flowers fell on her neck. She looked up at him with almost pitiful, scared grey eyes, wondering what he was doing. Flowers fell on her face, and she shut her eyes.

Suddenly, standing there above her, he felt awkward.

"I thought you wanted a funeral," he said, ill at ease.

Clara laughed strangely, and rose, picking the cowslips from her hair. She took up her hat and pinned it on. One flower had remained tangled in her hair. He saw, but would not tell her. He gathered up the flowers he had sprinkled over her. (pp. 280-81)

Because of this pagan ritual, Paul and Clara now engage in their first warm, spirited conversation—about a patch of bluebells poised in fear at the edge of the wood, like a man about to go outward into life, or like a woman about to enter the dark woods of love. Both images are clearly implied as the scene ends; both reveal character and situation, and on a deeper level, the poised flowers hint at one of Lawrence's favorite major themes—that Western man, living too much in the open spaces of the mind, must sooner or later confront the darker depths of emotion. And the key to all this revelation is how to pick flowers: Miriam, with false reverence; Paul with love, like a lover; and Clara not at all—but at least she respects the life in them, and later, when she is fully "awakened" by Paul, she will pick them, and the flowers, in their turn, will "defend" her.[7] All of which, if it proves nothing else, at least indicates that logic (in this case Mr. Aldington's logic) is not much of a match for the sure intuition of a creative artist.

III

But since flowers are the burden of this argument, the point must be pressed still further: the "picking scene" floods out to the rest of the book, that is, in either direction—backward, to the benedictive dust on Mrs. Morel's nose, or forward, to the first love scene between Paul and Clara, and to the final parting of Paul and Miriam in the closing paragraphs of the novel. For Paul, blessed by lily dust, must now claim the flower of life which caught in Clara's hair, and he must also place the flowers of death in Miriam's arms. In the first case, the scarlet carnations which he buys for Clara became an active force when he takes her on a trip to the countryside. Once there, the would-be lovers find a secluded spot near the bank of the Trent river, and for the first time they make love. The flowers give benediction to their union:

When she arose, he, looking on the ground all the time, saw suddenly sprinkled on the black, wet beech-roots many scarlet carnation petals, like splashed drops of blood; and red, small splashes fell from her bosom, streaming down her dress to her feet.

"Your flowers are smashed," he said. (p. 365)

The smashing works both ways, however, for this is the "baptism of fire in passion" which Paul has been seeking. Here too is the first sign of the vision of love which Lawrence would develop, in time, to full and confident expression as an ethic of renewal. Paul and Clara, because of their affair, will now come into their fullness as man and woman. And this is what Paul seems to be driving at, later on, when he explains to Miriam that Clara had been only half-alive with her husband, and that she needed to be fully awakened:

"That's what one *must have*, I think . . . the real, real flame of feeling through another person—once, only once, if it only lasts three months. See, my mother looks as if she'd *had* everything that was necessary for her living and developing. There's not a tiny bit of a feeling of sterility about her."

"No," said Miriam.

"And with my father, at first, I'm sure she had the real thing. She knows; she has been there. You can feel it about her, and about him, and about hundreds of people you meet every day; and, once it has happened to you, you can go on with anything and ripen."

"What has happened, exactly?" asked Miriam.

"It's so hard to say, but the something big and intense that changes you when you really come together with somebody else. It almost seems to fertilize your soul and make it that you can go on and mature."

"And you think your mother had it with your father?"

"Yes; and at bottom she feels grateful to him for giving it her, even now, though they are miles apart."

"And you think Clara never had it?"

"I'm sure." (pp. 372-73)

Paul's convictions are soon borne out: for once this "fertilization" process occurs, Clara is able to take back her husband, and Paul himself becomes man enough to resist the deathward pull from his mother's grave: "Together they had received the baptism of life; but now their missions were separate." The sign of this baptism, the active confirmation of it, was the scattering of red petals across their first bed—for the flowers *participated* in the mystery rite.

As the book ends, Paul makes his final break with Miriam, and even their last meeting, in his Nottingham rooms, is presided over by a bowl of freesias and scarlet anemones, "flaunting over the table." Because of the stifling nature of Miriam's love, Paul refuses to marry her. For her part, Miriam knows that "without him her life would trail on lifeless." But as they leave the rooms, Paul impulsively presents her with the flowers:

"Have them!" he said; and he took them out of the jar, dripping as they were, and went quickly into the kitchen. She waited for him, took the flowers, and they went out together, he talking, she feeling dead. (p. 490)

This final contrast between the two is again determined by their active and direct relation to a natural force. For Paul, who is emotionally vital, these are the flowers of life; for Miriam, who feeds wholly on the spirit and on personal affinity, they are the rootless flowers of death. Some fifteen years later, Lawrence would expand upon the general significance of Miriam's failure, using the same powerful floral imagery from this final scene in *Sons and Lovers:*

Oh, what a catastrophe, what a maiming of love when it was made a personal, merely personal feeling, taken away from the rising and the setting of the sun, and cut off from the magic connection of the solstice and the equinox! This is what is the matter with us. We are bleeding at the roots, because [like Miriam] we are cut off from the earth and sun and stars, and love is a grinning mockery, because, poor blossom, we plucked it from its stem on the tree of Life, and expected it to keep on blooming in our civilised vase on the table. ("A Propos of Lady Chatterley's Lover," *Sex, Literature and Censorship,* p. 109)

NOTES

1. Thus Lawrence defends this method in his foreword to *Women in Love:*

In point of style, fault is often found with the continual, slightly modified repetition. The only answer is that it is natural to the author; and that every natural crisis in emotion or passion or understanding comes from this pulsing, frictional to-and-fro which works up to culmination. (p. x)

2. The one outstanding exception to this statement is Dorothy Van Ghent, whose work on Lawrence appeared after the original composition of this manuscript. She speaks, for example, of the concrete reality of Lawrence's symbols, and of his passion "for the meaning of real things—for the individual expression that real forms have" (*The English Novel: Form and Function,* p. 248). She also finds some indications of the floral pattern in *Sons and Lovers* which confirm the material presented in this chapter. But since her explication is far from complete, and since it does not duplicate my theory of form and dimension in Lawrence's novels, I have preserved the present chapter more or less intact. I might also mention Frederick Hoffman's clear-headed (though in-

adequate) account of Lawrence's use of symbols, in *Freudianism and the Literary Mind:* "The symbol for Lawrence,"
he writes, "is merely the means by which the affective state
is kept alive—or the point at which it stores its latent energy,
awaiting new opportunities for discharge." He also calls it
the "fountain-source for all affective release" (pp. 178-79).

3. For a full account of the differences between Lawrence
and the symbolists, see my article, "Was D. H. Lawrence a
Symbolist," *Accent,* Winter 1955. To summarize its contents:
I argue that the symbolists try to evoke a timeless spiritual
absolute, so that their symbols function at the upper level of
language; whereas Lawrence works at the lower level of language and aims his symbols at the primitive indefinite. Beyond this radical divergence in language and metaphysics,
there is also an ontological cleavage—for the symbolist poem
moves toward non-being, while the Laurentian work of art
moves toward organic being, or at least upholds it. And
finally, on purely aesthetic grounds, symbolist art is always
static, while Laurentian art is unmistakably kinetic.

4. "Technique as Discovery," *Forms of Modern Fiction,*
ed. W. V. O'Connor. Mr. Schorer (who has since revised his
original estimate) feels that Lawrence simply states his
personal predicament in *Sons and Lovers,* and remains caught
in it without being able to resolve it, artistically. Yet the
floral pattern examined here decidedly ends in "artistic"
resolution.

5. *Aaron's Rod,* p. 273. Lawrence also speaks here of
Florence, the town of red lilies: "I reckon here men for a
moment were themselves, as a plant in flower is for the moment completely itself." This is the aloneness, the singleness
of being, which he prizes so much in *The Rainbow* and
Women in Love.

6. See especially pp. 47-48, 60. Dorothy Van Ghent also

clarifies some of the passages which Aldington misreads, in *The English Novel: Form and Function,* pp. 256-57. His obtuseness on this point suggests how willfully Lawrence (an angry and inconsistent man on many counts) has been blown up into the epitome of hopeless inconsistency.

7. This is precisely what happens when Lawrence groups the three again, this time in the Morel garden. Clara, who is now Paul's sweetheart, pulls a button from a hollyhock spire and breaks it to get the seeds: "Above her bowed head the pink flowers stared, as if defending her." Then Miriam arrives and, in the course of conversation, Paul tells his former sweetheart that the flowers in her yard are too sheltered: they "grow big and tender, and then die" (pp. 380-81).

4.

COUNTERFEIT LOVES

Sons and Lovers is interpreted, much too often, in terms of the "split" theory which Lawrence once outlined in a letter to Edward Garnett.[1] According to that letter, William and Paul Morel are unable to love normally when they come to manhood, because their dominant mother holds them back, so that a split occurs between body and soul—their sweethearts getting the former; their mother, the latter; while the boys themselves are shattered, inwardly, in the course of the struggle.

Admittedly, this theory accounts for much of the surface tension of the novel; but as Mark Schorer has pointed out, it seems to conflict with a second and wholly different scheme of motivation. Unless I am badly mistaken, this second scheme is more important than the first. For there seem to be *two* psychologies at work in *Sons and Lovers,* one imposed upon the other, though without destroying its effectiveness. We know, for example, that Lawrence had heard about Freud before he wrote the final draft of the novel.[2] We also know that the Garnett letter refers to the final draft, and that previous versions of the book had followed somewhat different lines. So Lawrence may well have written the book, at first, in accord with his own developing psychology, and then rewritten it in garbled accord with Freud's: hence the confusion, and the effect of superimposition, which bothers Mr. Schorer and many other readers. But if this is so, then the novel takes its strength from Lawrence's psychology and its weakness (inadvertently) from Freud's. The "split" theory, for example, is more Freudian than Laurentian; it involves a kind of Freudian triangle—mother-son-sweetheart—while the conflict in all future novels centers upon a single man and woman, a specific couple, whose relationship is judged or resolved in terms of its own vitality. We have already seen such conflicts, incidentally, in the floral scenes in *Sons and Lovers*, where vitality, or the full glow of the life-flame, is the chief criterion in Paul's specific relations with his mother, and with Miriam and Clara—where each affair is judged, in other words, in terms of its effect upon the life-flow, or the "livingness," of the man and woman involved. And as a matter of fact, each of Paul's three loves is actually significant in itself, since each contributes something vital to his development, yet finally proves destructive and inadequate. So all three loves—spiritual, oedipal, and possessive—resemble the counterfeit loves of later stories, and this in spite of the obvious Freudian twist which Lawrence seems to give them in his final draft.

Romantic Miriam Leivers, for example, with her love of intellect, her heavy dumb will, and her attempt to abstract the soul right out of Paul's body, has something in common with Hermione Roddice, that harsh creature of will and intellect in *Women in Love*. There is common ground, too, between what Clara Dawes wants out of Paul—possession, imprisoning personal love—and the princess-slave relationship in later stories like "The Captain's Doll." In the same vein, Mrs. Morel resembles the later and less appealing mothers in Lawrence's short stories (say, Pauline Attenborough in "The Lovely Lady," or Rachel Bodoin in "Mother and Daughter") who sap the life from their children, regardless of outside competition, because oedipal love is sterile in itself. The truth is, then, that *Sons and Lovers* is mainly an exploration of destructive or counterfeit loves—with a garbled Freudian "split" imposed upon it. At least this helps to explain the unique emotional tenor of the book: for in spite of all confusion there is a strange new reading experience here, a unique event in the realm of fiction, and in the realm of morality as well. Indeed, if *Sons and Lovers* is (as Harry Moore tells us) "the last novel of the nineteenth century," it is also one of the first novels of the twentieth. The book is only outwardly conventional; [3] it draws its greatest strength from Lawrence's radical new insight, moral as well as psychological, into the complex nature of emotional conflict.

II

Jessie Chambers cities a number of significant lines which appeared in the first draft of *Sons and Lovers,* but which were eliminated in the final version:

'What was it he (Paul Morel) wanted of her (Miriam)? Did he want her to break his mother down in him? Was that what he wanted?'

And again: 'Mrs. Morel saw that if Miriam could only win her son's sex sympathy there would be nothing left for her.' (*D. H. Lawrence: A Personal Record,* p. 191)

In the final draft of the book, and in Lawrence's letter to Garnett, this conflict is *stated* somewhat differently: if Miriam should win Paul's *soul,* then there would be nothing left for Mrs. Morel; as for his sex sympathy, the mother wants her to win that, if she will only leave his soul in her possession. Yet Lawrence makes it perfectly clear, through dramatic portions of the book, that Miriam's failure to attract Paul, physically, has led to her defeat in the spiritual conflict, and we see at once that the excised lines hold true to the actual situation. The girl's sexual failure is deeply rooted, for example, in her own emotional make-up. As Lawrence amply demonstrates, she is unable to lose herself in any simple pleasurable occasion, her body is tense and lifeless, her abnormal spiritual intensity is coupled with a genuine fear of things physical:

She walked with a swing, rather heavily, her head bowed forward, pondering. She was not clumsy, and yet none of her movements seemed quite *the* movement. Often, when wiping the dishes, she would stand in bewilderment and chagrin because she had pulled in two halves a cup or a tumbler. It was as if, in her fear and self-mistrust, she put too much strength into the effort. There was no looseness or abandon about her. Everything was gripped stiff with intensity, and her effort, overcharged, closed in on itself.

She rarely varied from her swinging, forward, intense walk. Occasionally she ran with Paul down the fields. Then her eyes blazed naked in a kind of ecstasy that frightened him. But she was physically afraid. If she were getting over a stile, she gripped his hands in a little hard anguish, and began to lose her presence of mind. And he could not persuade her to jump from even a small height. (pp. 182-83)

Lawrence even suggests the future sexual problem, in an early scene, when Miriam shows Paul the swing in her father's barn. Characteristically, she sacrifices the first turn to him, and he flies through the air, "every bit of him swinging, like a bird that swoops for joy of movement." Then he turns the swing over to the reluctant girl, and begins to set her in motion.

She felt the accuracy with which he caught her, exactly at the right moment, and the exactly proportionate strength of his thrust, and she was afraid. Down to her bowels went the hot wave of fear. She was in his hands. Again, firm and inevitable came the thrust at the right moment. She gripped the rope, almost swooning.

"Ha!" she laughed in fear. "No higher!"

"But you're not a *bit* high," he remonstrated.

"But no higher."

He heard the fear in her voice, and desisted. Her heart melted in hot pain when the moment came for him to thrust her forward again. But he left her alone. She began to breathe. (pp. 179-80)

Yet both Paul and Miriam are prudes in their early courtship. She recoils from "the continual business of birth and begetting" on the farm, and he takes his cue from her. Their own friendship is always pitched, moreover, at an intensely spiritual and intellectual level, so that even the simplest contact seems repellent: "His consciousness seemed to split. The place where she was touching him ran hot with friction. He was one internecine battle, and he became cruel to her because of it." Again, when the two chaste lovers are out for a walk one night, Paul suddenly stands transfixed at the sight of an enormous orange moon; his blood concentrates "like a flame in his chest," but this time Miriam shrinks away from actual contact: "it was as if she could scarcely stand the shock of physical love, even a passionate kiss, and then he was too shrinking and sensitive to give it."

Thus the chief "split" between Paul and Miriam comes from the abstract nature of their love, and not from the mother's hold upon the young man's soul. And the final responsibility for this split belongs with Miriam. When the friendship between the young couple wanes, for example, Paul resigns himself to the old love for his mother. But in the spring of his twenty-third year, he returns to the girl for another try at sensual love. This time, he seeks "the great hunger and impersonality of passion" with her, and though she agrees to this, she decides to submit herself religiously, as if to a sacrifice. Even as their love-making becomes more frequent, she continues to clench herself for the "sacrifice," as she had clenched herself on the swing in earlier days. So the lovers part once more, with this final confirmation that Miriam's frigidity is rooted in her own nature, and not in mere ignorance of sex. Her purity is nullity rather than innocence; she lacks real warmth, and Paul, in his youthful inexperience, is unable to rouse it in her. Although they meet again, after his mother's death, they are still divided by her incompleteness. Paul is shattered and adrift toward death himself; he wants her to respond to him out of warmth, out of womanly instinct. But she merely offers the old familiar sacrifice, and Paul rejects it:

"he did not hope to give life to her by denying his own."

Yet if Miriam lacks warmth, she has strength of will to spare. She endures Paul's insults, his cruel probings, his wrongheaded arguments; she lets him go, time and again, out of the conviction that she holds the ultimate key to his soul. And she does have the ability to stimulate him in his work, to arouse his own spiritual nature to fever pitch, and to serve as the necessary "threshing floor" for his ideas. Because of this ability, she believes "he cannot do without her"; but her belief results in a significant lapse—a kind of self-betrayal—when Paul decides to break away: "Always—it has always been so," she cries out. "It has been one long battle between us—you fighting away from me." The statement shocks Paul profoundly; he reasons that if she had known this all along, and had said nothing, then their love "had been monstrous."

He was full of a feeling that she had deceived him. She had despised him when he thought she worshipped him. She had let him say wrong things, and had not contradicted him. She had let him fight alone. . . . All these years she had treated him as if he were a hero, and thought of him secretly as an infant, a foolish child. Then why had she left the foolish child to his folly? His heart was hard against her. (p. 350)

The exposure of this duplicity (contempt disguised by reverence) shows Miriam in her truest colors. Quite plainly she resembles the willful Hermione Roddice of *Women in Love*, though she is never so poised, skillful, and predatory as Hermione. But the heavy dumb will is undeniably there, and this, coupled with her fierce desire to be a man, to succeed through intellectual knowledge, makes her a decided forerunner of those feminine creatures of intellect and will whom Lawrence would later deplore as spiritual vampires. Thus Miriam is a nun, in Paul's eyes, who would reduce the world to a nunnery garden: on the one hand, her excessive spirituality smothers his spirit; on the other, it destroys her own capacity to respond, sympathetically, to his newly-awakened need for sensual love.[4] And so she defeats herself in the struggle for Paul's heart, by thwarting his deep male instinct to be loved, impersonally, as a man, rather than as a mind or soul or personality. And she loses to Paul's mother by default, but she is not really defeated, at the deepest level of the conflict, by Mrs. Morel.

III

Nor is Clara Dawes defeated by Paul's mother, though she fits in better with the older woman's plans: she takes care of Paul's sexual needs, that is, and leaves plenty of him over for Mrs. Morel. So the mother is "not hostile to the idea of Clara"; in fact, she finds the relationship rather wholesome, after the soul-sucking affair with Miriam. She even likes Clara, but judges her as somehow not large enough to hold her son. Paul reaches a similar verdict about his mistress, independently, when he gives her back to her husband. But since Clara brings him a potentially fuller love than either Miriam or his mother, we must examine her role in the book with special care. She is, after all, the first imperfect version of the Laurentian woman, the "lost girl" in search of true womanhood.

Paul is 23 when he meets Clara, and she is about 30. He responds at once to her slumbering warmth, and senses that her aloofness is just a defensive pose. For her part, Clara admires his animal quickness: he brings her the promise of renewed vitality, and they draw close together and make love, once Paul has broken away from Miriam. Thus Paul receives the impersonal love he needs, "the real, real flame of feeling through another person," and Clara comes to full awakening as a woman. We can almost feel this transformation, for example, in a scene which follows their initial consummation in Clifton Grove. Now the lovers enter Clifton village, take tea at the house of an old lady, and rouse her to gaiety through their special warmth. As they are about to leave, the woman comes forward timidly "with three tiny

dahlias in full blow, neat as bees, and speckled scarlet and white."

She stood before Clara, pleased with herself, saying:

"I don't know whether—" and holding the flowers forward in her old hand.

"Oh, how pretty!' cried Clara, accepting the flowers.

"Shall she have them all?" asked Paul reproachfully of
the old woman.

"Yes, she shall have them all," she replied, beaming
with joy. "You have got enough for your share."

"Ah, but I shall ask her to give me one!" he teased.

"Then she does as she pleases," said the old lady,
smiling. And she bobbed a little curtsey of delight. (p.
367)

As her delight would seem to indicate, this is a
communion scene, and one which neatly affirms the
inward change in both of the lovers. The reward of
flowers, the life-symbol, to Clara is significant
enough; but it is the "true and vivid relationship"
with the old woman—her bright response to the lovers' mutual warmth—which gives us an immediate
sense of inward change. "By life," writes Lawrence,
"we mean something that gleams, that has the fourth-
dimensional quality" (*Phoenix,* p. 529).

In the months that follow, this "gleam" or fourth-
dimensional quality informs the relations between
Paul and Clara. When he pins berries on her coat,
she watches his quick hands, "and it seemed to her

she had never *seen* anything before. Till now, everything had been indistinct." When he embraces her,
she feels glad, erect, and proud again: "It was her
restoration and her recognition." She falls passionately in love with him, and he with her ("as far as
passion went"), till their love becomes an actual immersion in the "fourth dimension." One night, for instance, they take each other in an open field:

It was all so much bigger than themselves that he was
hushed. They had met, and included in their meeting the
thrust of the manifold grass-stems, the cry of the peewit,
the wheel of the stars. . . .

And after such an evening, they were both very still,
having known the immensity of passion. . . . To know
their own nothingness, to know the tremendous living
flood which carried them always, gave them rest within
themselves. If so great a magnificent power could over-
whelm them, identify them altogether with itself, so that
they knew they were only grains in the tremendous
heave that lifted every grass-blade its little height, and
every tree, and every living thing, then why fret about
themselves? They could let themselves be carried by
life, and they felt a sort of peace each in the other.
There was a verification which they had had together.
Nothing could nullify it, nothing could take it away; it
was almost their belief in life. (pp. 414-15)

Later on, Lawrence drops the "almost" out of that
final phrase, and develops his belief in life from
sexual love, or from the connection with the life-

force which sexual love implies. But in Sons and Lovers, his belief has barely taken shape, and the conflict between Paul and Clara is never well-defined. Nevertheless, the lines of definition are there, and Lawrence makes good use of them. Thus Clara is soon dissatisfied with impersonal love; like Miriam, she wants to grasp hold of Paul and to possess him personally. So she begins to crowd her love into the daytime hours at Jordan's factory. She presses Paul for little personal intimacies, but he shrinks away from this: "The night is free to you," he says. "In the daytime I want to be by myself. . . . Love-making stifles me in the daytime." But Paul is even more disturbed about another failing: he believes that Clara is unable to "keep his soul steady," that he is simply beyond her, in his creative and intellectual self, and in the breadth and depth of his emotional entanglement—which anticipates a later belief: that men and women must be in balance with each other, as individuals with distinct "life-flows" of their own, before genuine love can flourish. In Sons and Lovers, Clara falls short on this count: her "balance" with Paul is scarcely stable, and the growing uneasiness in their affair can be traced, for the most part, to her own inadequacy as an independent being. But even their common bond in passion begins to weaken, under this double burden of "imbalance" and possessive love:

They did not often reach again the height of that once when the peewits called. Gradually, some mechanical effort spoilt their loving, or, when they had splendid moments, they had them separately, and not so satisfactorily. . . . Gradually they began to introduce novelties, to get back some of the feeling of satisfaction. They would be very near, almost dangerously near to the river, so that the black water ran not far from his face, and it gave a little thrill; or they loved sometimes in a little hollow below the fence of the path where people were passing occasionally, on the edge of the town, and they heard footsteps coming, almost felt the vibration of the tread, and they heard what the passers-by said— strange little things that were never intended to be heard. And afterwards each of them was rather ashamed, and these things caused a distance between the two of them. (p. 427)

This disintegration in love is soon followed by an unexpected but climactic incident. Paul meets Clara's husband one night in a lonely field; Dawes has been waiting for him there and a wild battle follows, in which both opponents are badly damaged. Afterwards, the affair with Clara continues, but only on a mechanical plane: for Dawes has fought with the desperate strength of a man who wants his woman back, and Paul, for all his blind resistance, does not want the woman badly. And so he sheds his dying love in the battle, and a bit later on, he makes his restitution: he finds Dawes in the hospital

at Sheffield, befriends him, and gradually brings husband and wife together again.[5] Since Clara really
needs her stable, personal, daytime lover, she agrees
to the reunion. However that may be, she fails with
Paul because of her own shortcomings, for (along
with her possessiveness) she lacks the capacity, the
breadth of being, to take on the full burden of his
troubled soul.

IV

But if both Miriam and Clara defeat themselves, this
tells us something important about Mrs. Morel: it is
not her interference which destroys her sons, but the
strength and peculiar nature of her love. If we
switch for a moment to electrical terms, her sons are
drawn to her, away from the weaker poles of attraction, because she is the strongest force in the field—
and easily the most vital woman in the novel.[6] She
is warm and lively, for example, with those she loves,
for the early months with her husband were months
of passionate fulfillment. Though intellectual herself, she was first attracted to Morel by "the dusky,
golden softness of his sensuous flame of life"—and
this passion for manly, sensual men continues
throughout the book. She approves, for example, of
"the feel of *men* on things," and she takes imme-
diately to the good-looking Mr. Leivers. After her
first visit to his farm, she reveals a latent wish to the
young lad Paul: "Now *wouldn't* I help that man!

... *Wouldn't* I see to the fowls and the young stock. And *I'd* learn to milk, and *I'd* talk with him, and *I'd* plan with him. My word, if I were his wife, the farm would be run, I know!"

She also likes the quiet, compact miner, Mr. Barker, who takes good care of his pregnant wife, buys the week's groceries and meats on Friday nights, and keeps a level head. "Barker's little," she tells her husband, "but he's ten times the man you are." And the remark, however vindictive, holds true, for Morel has lost his manhood, and Lawrence gives us ample evidence of this throughout the novel. Unable to live up to his wife's high ideals, afraid of her mind, her will, and above all, her status as "that thing of mystery and fascination, a lady," Morel quarrels with her about money, he takes to drink, begins to mistreat her, and eventually, rather than face the problem in his own home, he retreats from the battle and breaks his own manhood. To be sure, there is a dual responsibility here, since Mrs. Morel has actually driven him to destroy himself. But the fact remains that Lawrence holds his men accountable, in the end, for their own integrity of being, and this will prove an important theme in future novels. The chief irony in *St. Mawr,* for example, is the lack of manhood in the modern world, which drives the heroine to preserve her horse, St. Mawr, as "the last male thing in the universe."

At this point in *Sons and Lovers,* Mrs. Morel turns

to her children for fulfillment. And here we run into one of the curious strengths of the book, for the companionship between mother and sons is described, at first, in completely wholesome terms. The destructive potential is there, of course, and Lawrence marks it out as he goes along; but on the whole this is a healthy relationship, and it remains so until the boys come of age. Thus William and Paul are actually kindled to life by their mother's affection; along with the other children, they love to gather about her to discuss the day's events; or they gather berries for Mrs. Morel; they bake bread, blanch walnuts, fetch the father's pay, and exult with her over bargains bought at the marketplace. Indeed, even when Paul falls sick and sleeps with his mother, Lawrence treats the occasion in terms of innocence and health:

> Paul loved to sleep with his mother. Sleep is still most perfect, in spite of hygienists, when it is shared with a beloved. The warmth, the security and peace of soul, the utter comfort from the touch of the other, knits the sleep, so that it takes the body and soul completely in its healing. Paul lay against her and slept, and got better; whilst she, always a bad sleeper, fell later on into a profound sleep that seemed to give her faith. (p. 82)

Thus, in spite of the general discord in the home, there is also a healthy side to the children's lives, and this helps to account, I think, for the delightful quality of the early scenes between Paul and his mother. On their trip to Nottingham, for instance, Mrs. Morel seems "gay, like a sweetheart," and the two of them feel "the excitement of lovers having an adventure together." But instead of two lovers, we see nothing more at Jordan's factory than an anxious mother and a shy, fumbling boy, who botches a "trial" translation for his potential employer. Paul finally gets the job, but there are still more embarrassing moments ahead: a long wait for a currant tart brings anguish to the pair; or their zest at a flower shop attracts the stares of its employees. But incidents like these are scarcely oedipal. There is the same sheer immersion in simple pleasures, for example, when Paul and his mother visit the Leivers' farm: on their way across the fields, they stop to admire a horse, a small truck, and a man silhouetted against the sky; Paul calls her attention to a heron floating above them; he jests at her clumsy manner of mounting stiles; and later, on the way home, their hearts ache with happiness. The early scenes between Paul and his mother are almost always like this—innocent, gay, full of warmth, and marked by lively talk.

But the tenor begins to change once William, the eldest son, dies in London of pneumonia and erysipelas. The death comes as a terrible blow to Mrs. Morel, who loved him passionately, and thought of him almost as "her knight who wore *her* favour in the battle." Now she loses all interest in life, and remains shut off from the family. But a few months later, Paul comes down with pneumonia too. "I should have watched the living, not the dead," she tells herself, and rouses her strength to save him:

Paul was very ill. His mother lay in bed at nights with him; they could not afford a nurse. He grew worse, and the crisis approached. One night he tossed into consciousness in the ghastly, sickly feeling of dissolution, when all the cells in the body seem in intense irritability to be breaking down, and consciousness makes a last flare of struggle, like madness.

"I s'll die, mother!" he cried, heaving for breath on the pillow.

She lifted him up, crying in a small voice:

"Oh, my son—my son!"

That brought him to. He realized her. His whole will rose up and arrested him. He put his head on her breast, and took ease of her love.

"For some things," said his aunt, "it was a good thing Paul was ill that Christmas. I believe it saved his mother." (pp. 167-68)

This scene is an important one, but it is not as oedipal as it seems. What Lawrence describes here is a legitimate communion, in his eyes. We have already seen the deeply positive stress which he places upon sleep with the beloved, and upon the healing qualities of loving touch. We have also seen the basic health of the mother-son relationship. Now that health is verified, for when Lawrence writes that

Paul "realized" his mother, he means that Paul has finally reached her, objectively, in valid, wholesome love. Paul is saved—saved, paradoxically, to be almost destroyed by the oedipal love which follows this event. For the beauty and richness of the scene is this: Lawrence has marshalled all the forces of destruction at precisely the same point at which he has just affirmed, dramatically, all that previous liveliness and love between Paul and his mother: William, the first son-lover, has been destroyed; now Paul will take his place in his mother's heart; he will *become* her second lover, he will in turn be sapped of his vitality, but at the moment he has just become her most beloved son.

In the years that follow, the relations between Paul and his mother are sometimes rich in satisfaction. He wins prizes for her with his artwork, and she looks upon them as part of her fulfillment. Paul sees it this way too: "All his work was hers." But there are quarrels over his love affairs, and Paul becomes increasingly unhappy. Then, late in the book, he finds "the quick of his trouble": he has loved both Miriam and Clara, but he can belong to neither of them while his mother lives; so long as she holds him, he can never "really love another woman." Thus Lawrence invokes the "split" theory, the pull between mother and sweethearts, to explain his hero's debilitation. But as we have already seen, this theory fails to account for the actual nature of Paul's affairs. We must look elsewhere, then, for the "quick" of his troubles; more specifically, we must look ahead to *Psychoanalysis and the Unconscious* (1921), where Lawrence was finally able to straighten out his views on oedipal love.

In this frontal attack on Freudian psychology, Lawrence decided that the incest-craving is never the normal outcome of the parent-child relationship, but always the result of impressions planted in the child's unconscious mind by an unsatisfied parent. But therefore oedipal love is mechanistic, and if mechanistic, then destructive and abnormal in itself. In one of the late stories, for example, an avaricious mother sends an unspoken whisper through her household—*There must be more money!*—and her young boy destroys himself in his attempts to get it. Now significantly enough, this pattern is already at work in *Sons and Lovers*, though here the whisper runs—*There must be fulfillment!*—as when Paul lies on the sofa, recovering from an early bout with bronchitis:

He, in his semi-conscious sleep, was vaguely aware of the clatter of the iron on the iron-stand, of the faint thud, thud on the ironing-board. Once roused, he opened his eyes to see his mother standing on the hearthrug with the hot iron near her cheek, listening, as it were, to the heat. Her still face, with the mouth closed tight from suffering and disillusion and self-denial, and her nose the smallest bit on one side, and her blue eyes so young, quick, and warm, made his heart contract with love. When she was quiet, so, she looked brave and rich with life, but as if she had been done out of her rights. It hurt the boy keenly, this feeling about her that she had never had her life's fulfilment: and his own incapability to make [it?] up to her hurt him with a sense of impotence, yet made him patiently dogged inside. It was his childish aim. (p. 80)

Here, then, is the planting of the incest germ, the unwitting imposition of the idea of fulfillment in the young boy's mind. Later on, when Paul becomes the actual agent of his mother's fulfillment, this idea leads inevitably to the incest-craving (through what Lawrence calls "a logical extension of the existent idea of sex and love," *Psychoanalysis*, p. 24), and from thence to the disintegration of his essential being. For the proof of this theory, take the constant wrangling with his mother; his fury at her old age; the almost violent quarrel with his father; his own mad restlessness; his obvious "will to die"; and, after the fight with Dawes, the complete blankness of his life. He is closer to his mother now than at any stage in the book, and the only thing which saves him from destruction is her own impending death. For Mrs. Morel falls ill with cancer now, and Paul cares for her, handling all the details with the doctors, as if he were the father. He is dazed and isolated from those around him; his grief stays with him like a mechanical thing which can't be shut off; he wants his mother to die, but she holds on to life, as always, with her powerful will; finally, he gives her an over-dose of morphia, and this kills her. He has openly played the lover in these last days, and his mother, though reduced to a strange, shrivelled-up little girl, is almost the young wife. But the very desperation of the situation gives it dignity: this is their special, private, intimate grief over an impossible dream, and the magnificence of the woman, and the devo-tional quality of Paul's love, render the deathbed scenes poignant and innocent.

Paul gives Clara back to her husband after this; he rejects Miriam, and is himself on the deathward drift, following his mother's spirit. And it is here, in the final pages, that his debilitation is most clearly the result, not of any split between mother and sweethearts, but of his powerful, sterile, obsessive and mechanistic love for his mother.

V

Thus, it is not the "split" theory which gives *Sons and Lovers* its marvelous power, but the successful dramatization of three destructive forms of love—oedipal, spiritual, and "unbalanced-possessive." It seems almost as if Paul were caught, at various times, within the swirling waters of three terrible whirl-pools, each of which drags him down toward a form

of death-in-life; and it is not so much the violent
shifts from one pool to the next which harm him, but
the damage he sustains within each separate pool:
and the most deathward swirl of them all is with his
mother.

These three disintegrative loves, when viewed separately, help to account for the emotional depth of
the book. But there is still Paul's "death" as a son to
account for, and his subsequent rebirth as a man,
which Lawrence dimly hints at in the final lines.
Paul is alone at night in the fields outside Nottingham, and wants only to follow his mother toward the
grave—

But no, he would not give in. Turning sharply, he
walked towards the city's gold phosphorescence. His fists
were shut, his mouth set fast. He would not take that direction, to the darkness, to follow her. He walked towards the faintly humming, glowing town, quickly.

As Harry Moore points out, Paul's return to life
hinges upon the final word, "quickly," which means
livingly rather than *rapidly*: "The last word in *Sons
and Lovers* is an adverb attesting not only to the
hero's desire to live but also to his deep ability to do
so." [7] And it is this quickness, this vitality, which has
enabled Paul to turn away, first from Miriam, then
Clara, and now, finally, from his mother. For if Paul
has failed in his three loves, he has also drawn from
them the necessary strength to live. We know, for

example, that Paul is a promising young artist, and Lawrence also tells us something significant about his art: "From his mother he drew the life-warmth, the strength to produce; Miriam urged this warmth into intensity like a white light." Now Clara must be considered, for she adds to this life-warmth and creative vision the gift of manhood, the "baptism of fire in passion" which will enable Paul "to go on and mature." Indeed, *nothing* can nullify this verification which he and Clara have had together—"it was almost their belief in life":

As a rule, when he started love-making, the emotion was strong enough to carry with it everything—reason, soul, blood—in a great sweep, like the Trent carries bodily its back-swirls and intertwinings, noiselessly. Gradually, the little criticisms, the little sensations, were lost, thought also went, everything borne along in one flood. He became, not a man with a mind, but a great instinct. His hands were like creatures, living; his limbs, his body, were all life and consciousness, subject to no will of his, but living in themselves. Just as he was, so it seemed the vigorous, wintry stars were strong also with life. He and they struck with the same pulse of fire, and the same joy of strength which held the bracken-frond stiff near his eyes held his own body firm. It was as if he, and the stars, and the dark herbage, and Clara were licked up in an immense tongue of flame, which tore onwards and upwards. Everything rushed along in living beside him; everything was still, perfect in itself, along with him.

This wonderful stillness in each thing in itself, while it was being borne along in a very ecstasy of living, seemed the highest point of bliss. (pp. 426-27)

This combination of hurling along in the sea of life, yet remaining still and perfect in oneself, is the nucleus of Laurentian belief, though we see here only a first rough version of things to come. Nevertheless, at the end of *Sons and Lovers*, we know, we have experienced the fact that Paul Morel has achieved a kind of half-realized, or jigsaw success, consisting of mixed elements of life-warmth, creative vision, incipient manhood, and most important of all, a belief (almost) in life itself: and this is the nutritive force which enables him, at the end, to become a man, and to turn quickly toward the glowing city, away from his mother.

NOTES

1. The letter is quoted and approved by Horace Gregory in *Pilgrim of the Apocalypse* and by Harry Moore in *The Life and Works of D. H. Lawrence*. It forms the basis of Mark Schorer's rather sharp attack on the novel, in "Technique as Discovery." Scraps and fragments of it appear in other studies, in the general effort to bolster purely Freudian readings of the novel. The most relevant passage follows:

A woman of character and refinement goes into the lower class, and has no satisfaction in her own life. She has had a passion for her husband, so the children are born of passion, and have heaps of vitality. But as her sons grow up, she selects them as lovers—first the eldest, then the second. These sons are *urged* into life by their reciprocal love of their mother—urged on and on. But when they come to manhood, they can't love, because their mother is the strongest power in their lives, and holds them. . . . As soon as the young men come into contact with women there is a split. William gives his sex to a fribble, and his mother holds his soul. But the split kills him, because he doesn't know where he is. The next son gets a woman who fights for his soul—fights his mother. The son loves the mother—all the sons hate and are jealous of the father. The battle goes on between the mother and the girl, with the son as object. The mother gradually proves the stronger, because of the tie of blood. The son decides to leave his soul in his mother's hands, and, like his elder brother, go for passion. Then the split begins to tell again. But almost unconsciously, the mother realizes what is the matter and begins to die. The son casts off his mistress, attends to his mother dying. He is left in the end naked of everything, with the drift towards death. (*Letters,* pp. 78-79)

As a number of critics have noted, there is at least one obvious discrepancy between the letter and the novel: at the end, Miriam takes the drift toward death, and Paul turns away from it.

2. In *Freudianism and the Literary Mind,* Frederick Hoffman quotes Frieda Lawrence to the effect that she and Lawrence had long arguments about Freud while Lawrence was preparing the final draft of *Sons and Lovers.* Hoffman suggests that these discussions led Lawrence to increase the emphasis upon the mother-son relationship, "to the neglect of other matters," but he feels that the book was "only super-

ficially affected" by Lawrence's introduction to Freud (p. 153).

3. One of the most deceptive aspects of the book, for example, is its apparent use of the class structure of the mining community as the realistic framework for the novel. This is in strict accord with nineteenth-century tradition. But except for the Leivers family, the members of the local community are only lightly sketched in. So the real framework for the novel becomes the Morel family itself, with Paul at its center: hence the book's original title, *Paul Morel*. But when Lawrence came to write about adult heroes, he could no longer utilize this natural structure, so he had to discover new forms —new patterns of experience—for the novel. Consider the parallel example of Thomas Wolfe, the American author, who was able to base *Look Homeward, Angel* on the life of his own family. Thus Eugene Gant is at the center of the novel, while his mother, father, and brother provide a "natural" framework around him. But when Wolfe moved to New York City, his novels became as formless as the sprawling fluid, complex medium in which he lived: hence the significance of one of his better stories, "Only the Dead Know Brooklyn." In their separate ways, both authors had plunged into the flux and formlessness of modern life; but unlike Lawrence, Wolfe was unable to give new order to his experience.

4. This concentrated attention on the lack of balance in Miriam's make-up (and its destructive consequences) seems to be the first clear-cut example of the psychology of organic being, or the "centers-of-consciousness" theory, which Lawrence would later work out, schematically, in *Psychoanalysis and the Unconscious*. The theory is a complicated one, but it does help to clarify the confused relationship between Paul and Miriam, so I will include a fuller explanation of it at this point. Lawrence divides the body into two upper spiritual poles and two lower sensual poles: at each of the two levels

there is a positive outward flow of sympathy and a negative assertion of will (the upper "will" achieves objective awareness of the beloved, while the lower "will" asserts the self). Now Miriam functions mainly on her upper poles, so that the flow of her spiritual sympathy tends to be excessive, or stifling, and her upper will is used for predatory ends. In the meantime, she has withered at the sensual level; she has no outward sensual flow (no warmth), nor can she assert her sensual independence (her proud womanhood): hence her touch proves sterile, and she can only feed upon Paul's vitality. All this should be taken figuratively, I think, as a coherent description of subjective human interchange. The scheme was derived *from* the novels, and it functions in them with remarkable flexibility.

5. The strange friendship between Dawes and Morel is one of the first significant male friendships in Lawrence's work. It is based on the attraction-repulsion scheme of all Laurentian loves, and the physical struggle seems to correspond with the famous wrestling scene in *Women in Love* (see Chapter 7). It should be noted, perhaps, that Dawes is as much the victim of an unjust woman as Walter (or for that matter, Paul) Morel, and this seems to be an important part of his appeal to Paul. Thus in Lawrence's first novel, *The White Peacock*, there is a similar bond of sympathy between two men who have suffered at the hands of women—the gamekeeper Annable, and the Lawrence-figure, Cyril Beardsall. For one obvious source of the friendship theme, see E. M. Forster's early novels, especially *Where Angels Fear to Tread* and *A Room with a View*.

6. Seymour Betsky reaches a similar conclusion in his contribution to *The Achievement of D. H. Lawrence: e.g.,* "the Morel sons realize that their mother is a considerably more remarkable woman than any they meet outside the home." His remarks on Mrs. Morel are especially perceptive, and

they also serve to affirm some of the material in this chapter. His work appeared, however, after the completion of this manuscript, and it differs from the present interpretation on many counts.

7. *Life and Works*, p. 105. Mr. Moore's observation stands in sharp contrast with Mark Schorer's contention, in "Technique as Discovery," that Paul returns to life "as nothing in his previous history persuades us that he could unfalteringly do." Yet there is nothing "unfaltering" about his final action: it is an act of will, and less a complete rebirth than a choice of direction, or the first stage of a potential resurrection. Nevertheless, it indicates his ascent to manhood, for the choice is clear and (as I try to show in the present chapter) extremely credible.

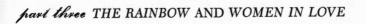

part three THE RAINBOW AND WOMEN IN LOVE

The road to excess leads to the palace of wisdom.

WILLIAM BLAKE

5.

THE SHAPE OF AN ARCH

A NUMBER of critics have seized upon the Cathedral as the dominant symbol of *The Rainbow,* as if there were no distinction between the pointed, or Gothic arch of the Cathedral, and the round arch of the rainbow.[1] Yet this distinction is central to the book, and it also marks an important new development in Lawrence's thought. In *Sons and Lovers,* for example, he had defined both Paul and Miriam in terms of arches.[2]

[Paul] talked to her endlessly about his love of horizontals: how they, the great levels of sky and land in Lincolnshire, meant to him the eternality of the will, just as the bowed Norman arches of the church, repeating themselves, meant the dogged leaping forward of the persistent human soul, on and on, nobody knows where; in contradiction to the perpendicular lines and to the Gothic arch, which, he said, leapt up at heaven and touched the ecstasy and lost itself in the divine. Himself, he said, was Norman, Miriam was Gothic. She bowed in consent even to that. (p. 210)

93

And so must the reader bow in consent, since Miriam's nature is intensely spiritual, and Paul's outlook, his belief in the sweep of life, is intensely pagan. What we see, then, in *Sons and Lovers,* is an embryonic conflict between two religious concepts: namely, the spiritual infinite and the primitive indefinite—the Gothic and the "Norman" arch, the Cathedral and the rainbow, or to push on a little toward our final chapter, Christ Risen in the Spirit and Christ Risen, glad and whole, in the Flesh. This conflict is at the core of *The Rainbow,* it is echoed in *Women in Love,* and is, indeed, never wholly absent from any of the novels.

Yet it is not precisely an "either-or" conflict, as some critics would have us believe. Rather, it is a conflict between two different versions of the *whole* of life. Take the strange double criticism which goes on in *The Rainbow,* for instance, of the flesh as well as the spirit. This criticism is prepared for in the opening lines.

The Brangwens had lived for generations on the Marsh Farm, in the meadows where the Erewash twisted sluggishly through alder trees, separating Derbyshire from Nottinghamshire. Two miles away, a church-tower stood on a hill, the houses of the little country town climbing assiduously up to it. Whenever one of the Brangwens in the fields lifted his head from his work, he saw the church-tower at Ilkeston in the empty sky. So that as he turned again to the horizontal land, he was aware of something standing above him and beyond him in the distance.

The rising tower, then, and the horizontal farm-land, are the two "elements" which will be criticized in the novel: for the one represents an outworn form of spirituality, and the other, an inadequate, mind-less immersion in the teeming life of the farm. But at the same time, both elements—vertical and hori-zontal, spiritual and sensual—will contribute to the symbol which *relates* them both: the rainbow, the symbol of a new kind of oneness with the Infinite, (or more accurately, with the "twofold" Infinite), and of a new kind of "holy knowledge." [3]

For it is the thrust outward from the farm, in quest of "twofold" knowledge, which constitutes the central theme of the novel: the Brangwen women want something more than mere "blood-intimacy" with the life around them; they look outward, be-yond the farm, to the "far-off world of cities and gov-ernments . . . where men moved dominant and cre-ative, having turned their back on the pulsing heat of creation . . . whereas the Brangwen men faced inwards to the teeming life of creation, which poured unresolved into their veins." The women seek some "higher form of being" than unresolved blood-inti-macy, some "finer, more vivid circle of life" for their children, and the novel revolves around this search by three generations of the Brangwen family. In the course of their quest, the "self in its wholeness" must be formed and fulfilled, and new religious modes must be discovered.

As the novel opens, for example, Tom Brangwen begins to search for a better life than the farm will give him. He is a sensitive boy, "more sensuously developed" than those around him, but slow and confused when it comes to "deliberate learning." In the home, his mother has always been the fount and symbol of love, religion, and morality. Now Tom seeks another woman to perform this function for him—to serve, in effect, as an anchor for his soul. About five years after his mother's death, he meets a Polish widow, Lydia Lensky, who seems to possess the strength and refinement which he seeks. Appropriately enough, their first brief conversation occurs in the Brangwen farm kitchen, where his mother had formerly held sway. Tom is sure of himself here, and the Polish woman gives him even greater confidence. He proposes to her, a short time later, in *her* kitchen at the local vicarage, and she agrees to the marriage. As F. R. Leavis has observed, this foreign woman brings "otherness" and self-possession to the Brangwens. Indeed, she seems so strange to Tom, so aloof and self-contained, that he begins to move away from her, in the second year of their marriage, in search of a mistress. But Lydia recognizes the threat at once; she pulls him back and challenges him to active love. In the sexual consummation which follows, they discover and affirm each other's independent being; then each goes his own way again, transfigured, separate, yet firmly bound together as the other's gateway to life.[4] And it is Lydia's "otherness" which makes this consummation possible—which forces Brangwen to assert and then establish his own identity, his essential separateness of being. Almost 25 years later, her function for Tom and for the whole family remains the same:

She seemed always to haunt the Marsh rather than to live there. She was never part of the life. Something she represented was alien there, she remained a stranger within the gates, in some ways fixed and impervious, in some ways curiously refining. She caused the separateness and individuality of all the Marsh inmates, the friability of the household. (p. 227)

Yet Tom's fulfillment is only partial. At 45 he feels unfinished, unestablished. He is vital in himself, he has known fully "the long marital embrace with his wife," but he has also missed out on an important part of life. In the early days, for instance, when his love with his wife had seemed inadequate, he had turned to her daughter, Anna, with the secret wish to make the girl a lady—to give her the further "creative life" which he first desired for himself, under the influence of his mother. Now, at 45, Tom still desires this life, but Anna's marriage to Will Brangwen, his nephew, marks the end of his own development.

His work on the farm seems insignificant, and though he shares his wife's belief in a vague and indefinable God, he is still afraid of the "unknown," still unformed at the time of his death.

II

In the next generation, Anna and Will Brangwen continue the quest for twofold knowledge. Will brings together in imperfect union such family traits as "blood-intimacy" and religious aspiration. Anna performs her mother's former role: proud and independent by nature, she forces Will to an even more marked assertion of his separateness than his uncle's. All through the first years of their marriage, she resists the absorbing, willful quality of her husband's love. In the end she defeats him, and the home life continues on a matriarchal basis. She rules him, along with a growing brood of children, in the practical daytime world, and though she learns to love him at night, she fails to respect him.

But Will is soon dissatisfied with his lot, so he begins to slip off by himself. One night he meets a childish, vulnerable girl in a Nottingham theatre, and proceeds to seduce her. She is merely "the sensual object of his attention," and the problem is to overpower her through force of will and cold, sensual attraction; but at the last moment his hatred for the girl wells up, and he is unable to take her. Nevertheless, the experience sets Will apart from his old self. When he returns home, Anna rouses instantly to the change in him; she provokes him to an even higher pitch than her Nottingham rival, and for a time she and her husband abandon themselves to a passionate duel of sensual discovery:

It was as if he were a perfect stranger, as if she were infinitely and essentially strange to him, the other half of the world, the dark half of the moon. She waited for his touch as if he were a marauder who had come in, infinitely unknown and desirable to her. And he began to discover her. He had an inkling of the vastness of the unknown sensual store of delights she was. With a passion of voluptuousness that made him dwell on each tiny beauty, in a kind of frenzy of enjoyment, he lit upon her: her beauty, the beauties, the separate several beauties of her body.

He was quite ousted from himself, and sensually transported by that which he discovered in her. He was another man revelling over her. There was no tenderness, no love between them any more, only the maddening, sensuous lust for discovery and the insatiable, exorbitant gratification in the sensual beauties of her body. And she was a store, a store of absolute beauties that it drove him mad to contemplate. There was such a feast to enjoy, and he with only one man's capacity. (p. 221)

The duel continues for some time. They revel in one another, as Tom Brangwen and his wife had revelled before them, and as Rupert and Ursula (Brangwen) Birkin would revel after them, in order to root out all shame, all fear of the body's secrets: "They accepted shame, and were one with it in their most unlicensed pleasures. It was incorporated. It was a bud that blossomed into beauty and heavy, fundamental gratification."

Here Lawrence seems to find a place, in marriage, for cold, lustful desire (as opposed, apparently, to "hot, living desire"); and its function—a limited one —is discovery and purification: a sensual revel, a phallic "hunting out" which leaves one free for the deeper, warmer love he generally upholds.[5] But more than this, the experience sets Brangwen free to attend to his public tasks, which he had hitherto endured as so much mechanical activity. Now his purposive self is roused and released, and he begins at 30 to teach woodwork classes at the Cossethay night-school. About ten years later he returns to his own creative work in wood and other materials, and soon afterwards he receives an appointment as Art and Handwork Instructor for the County of Nottingham. Through the purgation process, both he and his wife have been aroused to active, purposive life— she, from the long sleep of motherhood; he, from social sterility to a point of social and self-respect.

So there is a decided connection, in Lawrence's world, between love and creative labor, between satisfaction of the deepest sensual self and a more spiritual form of satisfaction. Hence Brangwen's struggle toward self-responsibility is tied in, intimately, with the two elements which Lawrence wants to criticize in the novel: with the church spire and the horizontal farmland, or with the Christian infinite and the Brangwen immersion in blood-intimacy. Once Will asserts his independent self, for example, he is able to curb his *absorbing* sensual ways, and to enjoy that deep impersonal love which sets him free for creative labor. But along with this, he must also free himself from the kind of religious life which the church provides him; and in this respect the critique of Christian spiritualism seems quite pertinent: for the affair between Will and Anna really begins with his Ruskin-like love of church architecture, and centers around his passionate involvement in religious mystery. On the day they meet, Anna bursts out laughing in church at the loud sincerity of Will's clear tenor. But she is also carried away to the outside world, as Will speaks passionately to the family about nave and chancel, about Gothic, Norman and Renaissance architecture. Then, in the first luxurious weeks of their marriage, they begin to quarrel about religion. Anna has rejected orthodoxy by this time: soul and self are one with her, and she wants something more than the call to social duty issued by the church. Consequently, she resents the fact that Will moves freely, like an escaped and *selfless* soul, among the mysterious vaults of the church; she begins to jeer at him and to fire away at his half-articulate beliefs with all the ammunition which nineteenth-century rationalism can provide. But the quarrel is soon resolved, on other grounds, during a visit to Lincoln Cathedral. As the young couple enters, Will's soul leaps into the great vaults ("His body stood still, absorbed by the height"), to consummation at the apex of the arch.

Here the stone leapt up from the plain of earth, leapt up in a manifold, clustered desire each time, up, away from the horizontal earth, through twilight and dusk and the whole range of desire, through the swerving, the declination, ah, to the . . . meeting, the clasp, the close embrace, the neutrality, the perfect, swooning consummation, the timeless ecstasy. There his soul remained, at the apex of the arch, clinched in the timeless ecstasy, consummated.

And there was no time nor life nor death, but only this, this timeless consummation, where the thrust from earth met the thrust from earth and the arch was locked on the keystone of ecstasy. This was all, this was everything. Till he came to himself in the world below. Then again he gathered himself together, in transit, every jet of him strained and leaped, leaped clear into the darkness above, to the fecundity and the unique mystery, to the touch, the clasp, the consummation, the climax of eternity, the apex of the arch. (p. 190)

Anna too is roused by the cathedral, but she also feels roofed in by it. She knows that the open sky outside has somehow been excluded from this timeless place, and so, spying the wicked little faces carved on the cathedral wall, she seizes on these to prevent her soul from being swept aloft.

These sly little faces peeped out of the grand tide of the cathedral like something that knew better. They knew quite well, these little imps that retorted on man's own illusion, that the cathedral was not absolute. They winked and leered, giving suggestion of the many things that had been left out of the great concept of the church. "However much there is inside here, there's a good deal they haven't got in," the little faces mocked.

Apart from the lift and spring of the great impulse towards the altar, these little faces had separate wills, separate motions, separate knowledge, which rippled back in defiance of the tide, and laughed in triumph of their very own littleness. (p. 191)

The choice of the "little faces" seems most appropriate here. In the previous century, John Ruskin had also chosen them as "constitutional ornaments," as the creative products, that is to say, of "healthy and ennobling labour":

Go forth again to gaze upon the old cathedral front, where you have smiled so often at the fantastic ignorance of the old sculptors: examine once more those ugly goblins, and formless monsters, and stern statues, anatomiless and rigid; but do not mock at them, for they are signs of the life and liberty of every workman who struck the stone; a freedom of thought, and rank in scale of being, such as no laws, no charters, no charities can secure; but which it must be the first aim of all Europe at this day to regain for her children. (*The Stones of Venice*, II, p. 163)

Thus it is Ruskin's concept of the dignity and wholeness of each separate workman which Anna seems to emphasize. And in the argument which follows, Will Brangwen comes to see her point. Somewhere inside him he responds "more deeply to the sly little faces that knew better, than he had done before to the perfect surge of the cathedral." Then too, he sees that the life outside contains something great and free, joyous and careless, which the church no longer includes. And so he loses his hold on the absolute. Yet he continues to love the church as a symbol for something old, sacred and familiar, and he becomes, quite literally, the caretaker of the little church near his home: "He tended it for what it tried to represent rather than for that which it did represent."

And that is the whole point: the church is a dominant symbol in *The Rainbow* only as it represents something else—namely, the rainbow, the symbol for a different kind of absolute which the church can only imply, indirectly, for Will and Anna, and later for their daughter Ursula. And if we move on to the "phallic hunt" already mentioned, this is precisely what Lawrence tells us with regard to Will's experience:

He had always, all his life, had a secret dread of Absolute Beauty. It had always been like a fetish to him, something to fear, really. For it was immoral and against mankind. So he had turned to the Gothic form, which always asserted the broken desire of mankind in its pointed arches, escaping the rolling, absolute beauty of the round arch.

But now he had given way, and with infinite sensual violence gave himself to the realization of this supreme, immoral, Absolute Beauty, in the body of woman. It seemed to him, that it came to being in the body of woman, under his touch. Under his touch, even under his sight, it was there. (pp. 222-23)

There is no attempt, in this passage, to substitute the sensual consummation for Christianity. Instead, Lawrence is indicating a path toward a fuller religious life than the church can offer Brangwen: he connects this sensual experience with other positive and (in his eyes) essentially religious aspects of Brangwen's life—his release to the more spiritual realm of creative labor, the establishment of his separate self, his fulfillment as an individual and his wife's fulfillment as well. It should be emphasized, moreover, that this fulfillment is extremely limited for both of them: they do not arrive at the "rainbow condition" in this novel, nor is there any real scope or spaciousness in their lives; consequently, the Will Brangwen who appears in *Women in Love* is a confused and incoherent man of 50, "a roomful of old echoes," as unresolved and uncreated as he was at 20. This is not inconsistency on Lawrence's part, but an honest comment upon Brangwen's failure to articulate new values: if Will and his wife have emerged as separate beings, if both have had their satisfactions, neither has reached that stage of proud, *conscious* being which Lawrence was then attempting to formulate for himself.

III

Ursula Brangwen fares better, in this respect, than either of her parents, since she inherits or acquires their strongest qualities. In her the "otherness" and refinement of the Lensky strain is finally fused, by blood, with the sensual warmth and the deep religiosity of the Brangwens. She is also her father's daughter, as Anna was her foster-father's daughter, and as Tom Brangwen was his mother's favorite son —and Lawrence makes it clear that the impetus toward fuller life is always passed along from parent to child, through close emotional contact. Thus Ursula looks for men who will lead her outward, toward creative life, just as Anna saw Will Brangwen as a door to the outside world, and to switch sexes, just as Tom Brangwen sought refinement through Lydia Lensky. But Ursula will reach a much higher point of fulfillment, in this general groping outward, than her predecessors. She will fight all her major battles *before* marriage rather than after, and thereby solve some of the major problems which prevented full development in Will and Anna, in Tom and Lydia Brangwen: the lack of scope and purpose in life; fear of the unknown; the side-track into Christianity; and finally, the lapse into the "violent trance" of ordinary motherhood. Like Alvina Houghton in *The Lost Girl*, Ursula will reject the conventional frame of life, she will cut herself off from its social and religious guide ropes and will become a "lost girl" herself, as the novel ends, though she will eventually find herself, in *Women in Love*, through marriage with Rupert Birkin.

In the meantime there is the problem, in *The Rainbow*, of sloughing off the ties which bind her to ordinary life. She revolts, first of all, from the fecund, chaotic atmosphere of her home, and finds peace, singleness, and a sense of the past through talks with her grandmother at the Marsh Farm. She escapes next from the levelling pull of village life by attending school in Nottingham. Later she revolts from the church. From her father, she has received her first intimation of religious mystery, and of the dark sensual underworld where Brangwen reigns so potently. Now she looks for these things in the Christian religion, and she lives for a while in the passionate, visionary realm of the church. But gradually the world of fact begins to obtrude upon this realm: she objects to the emphasis upon sin, she finds fault with the humble side of Christianity, and she tries to find some weekday meaning for religious passion. But failing to find it, her religion becomes "a tale, a myth, an illusion," and the church itself becomes, as with her father, a symbol for something it has "tried to represent, rather than for that which it did represent." In her early courtship with Skrebensky, for example, the two of them look into the large church at Derby which is then under repair: there are bits of plaster falling upon them, dust floats through the air, the secular shouts of workmen ring out coarsely through the aisles—and Ursula sees herself and Skrebensky as two travelers, clambering on unhurt as the world tumbles in ruins about them. Later, when their affair is at its peak, they visit the cathedral at Rouen, and its majestic stability reminds her of "something she had forgotten and wanted." This proves to be the turning point in their affair, for Skrebensky, like the church, has been unable to provide her with a valid sense of the "unknown."

Ursula explores and exhausts still other realms of experience in her search for "higher being." During her school days she decides to succeed in the "man's world of daily work and duty," but she is soon caught up in a lesbian affair with Winifred Inger, one of her instructors. Then the heavy, cleaving deadness of the affair disgusts her, so she marries the woman off to her homosexual uncle, Tom Brangwen (junior), who manages a colliery in Yorkshire. When the two women visit him there, Ursula is further sickened by the monstrous colliery system, which reduces men to mere instruments and spreads its squalid blight across the countryside. Tom and Winifred revile this system too, yet serve it to escape their own perversity; and this is typical of Lawrence's social insight—this lumping together of inverted lovers with an industrial system which dehumanizes its adherents: hence in *Women in Love*, the perverted artist, Loerke, reduces even art to the interpretation of industry, in terms of pure motion and service to the machine, with the human element left out.

This "nullification" theme begins, however, in *The Rainbow*. When Ursula teaches school, for example, she is forced to treat her students as objects rather than human beings, and to govern them through sheer force of disciplinary will. Later she attends college "to hear the echo of learning pulsing back to the source of the mystery"; but she finds that even the college has been converted to a sham workshop for industry and science.

"No, really [a woman physicist tells her], I don't see why we should attribute some special mystery to life— do you? We don't understand it as we understand electricity, even, but that doesn't warrant our saying it is something special, something different in kind and distinct from everything else in the universe—do you think it does? May it not be that life consists in a complexity of physical and chemical activities, of the same order as the activities we already know in science? I don't see, really, why we should imagine there is a special order of life, and life alone—" (p. 416)

But Ursula finds mystery even in the one-celled animal which wiggles on the plate of her microscope: not a mechanical physico-chemical thing endowed with a few biological urges, but a consummation, a being infinite: "Self was a oneness with the infinite," she decides. "To be oneself was a supreme, gleaming triumph of infinity."

"Self was a oneness with the infinite"—here Lawrence invokes a basic "law" of life, inherent in *Sons and Lovers*, but articulated now, for the first time, as the motivating principle of *The Rainbow*, of *Women in Love*, and of the vast bulk of the work which follows. Like the famous Laurentian flower, with its roots thrust deep in the nourishing earth, with its face uplifted in perfect singleness, Ursula must reach true being through life-giving contact with the "infinite." But again it is a question of the "twofold" infinite, or as I have called it, the twofold "primitive indefinite": for both flesh and spirit are involved in Ursula's relations with Anton Skrebensky, the poised and self-possessed young son of a Polish baron and an English lady, who will lead her outward (she believes) to the new life of greater self-realization and "plunging, boundless freedom."

From the first, however, the terms of this life are confused and inadequate in Ursula's mind. She thinks of the self, for instance, as the old, finite personal self which Lawrence had specifically abandoned in his conception of *The Rainbow:* "You mustn't look in my novel for the old stable ego of the character," he wrote to Edward Garnett. "There is another ego, according to whose action the individual is unrecognizable, and passes through, as it were, allotropic states which it needs a deeper sense than any we've been used to exercise, to discover are states of the same radically-unchanged element" (*Letters,* p. 200). This "radically-unchanged element" is the real self which Lawrence identifies, almost, with the soul, for as Anna Brangwen puts it, self and soul are one, or should be one.[6] Thus Lawrence insists here on the uniqueness of the individual soul—a confusing point, perhaps, but if we look ahead to *Women in Love* we find a helpful argument: equality of spirit is a falsehood, says Rupert Birkin; spiritually there is pure difference, intrinsic otherness, between one man and the next. But Ursula still caters to the finite, "personal" self, and so neglects the basic needs of her second, "impersonal" self, which Lawrence identifies with the soul. Take this revealing passage, on her love-making with Skrebensky:

It was a magnificent self-assertion on the part of both of them, he asserted himself before her, he felt himself infinitely male and infinitely irresistible, she asserted herself before him, she knew herself infinitely desirable, and hence infinitely strong. And after all, what could either of them get from such a passion but a sense of his or her own maximum self, in contradistinction to all the rest of life? Wherein was something finite and sad, for the human soul at its maximum wants a sense of the infinite. (pp. 284-85)

So it is the self, cut off from the rest of life, which Ursula tries to affirm, and her fierce desire for "burning consummation with the infinite" is really an assertion of triumph over the rest of life, rather than conjunction with it. As Lawrence tells us in *Women in Love,* Ursula is a modern girl, a sister of Artemis, the virgin huntress, the moon goddess who protects all women; and she is also a daughter of Aphrodite, whom Lawrence calls the goddess of dissolution and death. Thus, when Ursula seeks consummation with the moon, she asserts the principle of the triumphant female, and this is the broader meaning of the two strange moon scenes in *The Rainbow.* In each of these scenes, she taunts Skrebensky to take her under the cold, harsh moonlight, and though he complies, he feels each time that some sort of proof is being put upon him and that death is the penalty for failure. At the same time, Skrebensky is really unable to lead the girl to a fuller existence. Ursula comes to sense this inadequacy; she knows, instinctively, that the man is null at the core of his being and content with his own instrumentality. As a soldier, he devotes himself to the good of the greatest number and counts his intrinsic self as nothing. "I belong to the nation," he tells her, "and must do my duty by the nation." But since Ursula sees the nation as a mechanical, commercial monster, she answers him harshly: "It seems to me . . . as if you weren't anybody—as if there weren't anybody there, where you are. Are you anybody, really? You seem like nothing to me." And she proceeds, quite unconsciously, to destroy him with corrosive love.

But first they enjoy an interlude of rich consummation—an initiation to life. Skrebensky returns to England after a few years of service in South Africa. He seems to possess the darkness of that continent in his blood, and as the affair with Ursula resumes, he enriches her with "living darkness." Ursula gains freedom and separate strength from the experience, and Skrebensky too seems flooded with new life. But as the affair wears on, his nullity in the daytime world becomes apparent; he feels completely empty when alone, and breaks down in tears when Ursula rejects his offer of marriage. Like Gerald Crich in *Women in Love*, Skrebensky has been aroused and exposed to life, but seems unable to support himself beyond a woman's orbit. In other words, he fails to lead a creative, purposive existence of his own, and apparently his failure here, in the realm of spiritual satisfaction, has cancelled out the significance of his sensual enrichment. As Ursula sums it up: "She knew him all round, not on any side did he lead into the unknown. Poignant, almost passionate appreciation she felt for him, but none of the dreadful wonder, none of the rich fear, the connection with the unknown, or the reverence of love." A short while later she pins him down upon her, under an incandescent moon, and breaks his soul in her fierce desire to reach the blazing unknown: moon and woman together test, expose, penetrate and destroy his inadequate manhood. Skrebensky marries another girl, a few weeks later, and sails with her for India.

But Ursula is also shattered by the experience. Now pregnant by Skrebensky, her emotions gather within her, the tension mounts, then breaks its bounds, one day, in the form of a vision: as she walks through the woods during a rainstorm, wild horses bear down upon her with their trampling hooves; she flees them, narrowly escapes, returns home, and takes to her bed with a raging fever; in the delirium which follows she casts off the embryo within her and thus burns out the last trace of Skrebensky.[7] Then, as the book ends, she begins to feel newborn, like a kernel "free and naked and striving to take new root, to create a new knowledge of Eternity in the flux of Time." In the distance, a rainbow seems to form, as a sign of this new knowledge:

And the rainbow stood on the earth. She knew that the sordid people who crept hard-scaled and separate on the face of the world's corruption were living still, that the rainbow was arched in their blood and would quiver to life in their spirit, that they would cast off their horny covering of disintegration, that new, clean, naked bodies would issue to a new germination, to a new growth, rising to the light and the wind and the clean rain of heaven. She saw in the rainbow the earth's new architecture, the old, brittle corruption of houses and factories swept away, the world built up in a living fabric of Truth, fitting to the over-arching heaven.

F. R. Leavis calls *The Rainbow* an unfinished book (he also calls it "a major work of a great writer"), because this ending seems too arbitrary and declaratory, in his eyes. Yet the ending holds true enough, I think, since Ursula Brangwen becomes a woman in these final pages, in the same way, essentially, as Paul Morel is born as a man at the end of *Sons and Lovers*. She too has cast off all the shackles of the past, she too has been roused to life through baptismal love, and even more clearly than Paul, she has taken root in the "unknown." She knows, for example, that a man created by God will come to her out of the Eternity "to which she herself belongs," and clearly the rainbow is, in part, a sign that she is ready for fulfillment. One might quarrel, perhaps, with the social optimism of this final passage; yet Lawrence's meaning rings true, at the least, to that new and fuller vision of life whose elements—blood-intimacy, self-responsibility, the sensual fires, polarity in love, creative labor, spiritual uniqueness, and the sacred nature of human interchange—are so conspicuously present in this and all his future novels.

NOTES

1. Horace Gregory uses the two arches interchangeably in *Pilgrim of the Apocalypse,* pp. 33-38. He also sees the cathedral scene as "a symbol of marriage as a religious experience, a symbol of a particular kind of transcendentalism that was to find its rapid growth in Lawrence's philosophy" —which is precisely what it is not. In the *Kenyon Review,* Winter 1941, Eliseo Vivas treats Lawrence like a latter-day Walter Pater: he speaks of the cathedral experience as one of "pure ecstasy," and equates it with all other "halcyon moment[s] of pure consciousness" in Lawrence's work. In *The English Novel: Form and Function,* Dorothy Van Ghent makes the more common error: "In other novels, the arch of a rainbow and the arches of a church form images with which are associated the aspiration toward a selfhood that is in rhythm with natural forces and yet integral in form." (p. 458) But the cathedral arch really excludes the natural world, and Will Brangwen's aspiration towards it is unmistakably *selfless.*

2. Jessie Chambers (*i.e.,* Miriam Leivers) gives us the background for this passage in her *D. H. Lawrence: A Personal Record* (by E. T.). She and Lawrence often studied together in the privacy of his home:

We talked of many things besides French once the door was closed and there arose the magical sense of being alone together. We tried to find out the differences in our own characters. Lawrence told me that I was high and very deep, whereas he was very broad but comparatively shallow.

'It's like this,' he said, taking a piece of chalk from his pocket and drawing spirals on the board below the mantel-shelf. 'Your impulse is to go higher and higher, towards perfection, and mine is to go forward, on and on, for aeons and aeons. . . .'

'What is an aeon?' I asked.

'Time past all reckoning. Beyond for ever and ever,' he replied with shining eyes. (p. 56)

3. Lawrence's terminology is often terribly misleading, but it is at least possible to grasp the general nature of his meta-physics. By the "infinite" he usually means what I would call the primitive indefinite. But he seems to endow this concept with spiritual as well as sensual properties, so that there is actually a twofold approach to the ineffable in his novels. The spiritual consummation, for example, comes through "passionate, purposive activity" (rather than prayer), and the sensual consummation comes through the act of love. In the present novel, the rainbow serves to relate and keep distinct these *interdependent* modes of consummation. In other words, it is a sign of the self in its wholeness, or of the "Holy Ghost" which Lawrence writes about in his theoretical works. And it is this concept, this total experience, which he sets against the exclusive *selflessness* of the Christian con-summation, at the apex of the Gothic arch. It is true, of course, that "passionate, purposive activity" is also selfless; but it functions (paradoxically) as part of the greater process of Laurentian self-fulfillment. Take this revealing quotation,

from *Twilight in Italy* (which was written in conjunction with *The Rainbow*), on the dual nature of Laurentian fulfillment:

> It is past the time to cease seeking one Infinite, ignoring, striving to eliminate the other. The Infinite is twofold, the Father and the Son, the Dark and the Light, the Senses and the Mind, the Soul and the Spirit, the self and the not-self. . . . The consummation of man is twofold, in the Self and in Selflessness. . . . And man must know both.

> But he must never confuse them. They are eternally separate. . . . They are always opposite, but there exists a relation between them. This is the Holy Ghost of the Christian Trinity . . . which relates and keeps distinct the dual natures of God. To say that the two are one, this is the inadmissible lie. The two are related, by the intervention of the Third, into a Oneness. . . . And in the Holy Spirit I know the Two Ways, the Two Infinites, the Two Consummations. And knowing the Two, I admit the Whole. But excluding One, I exclude the Whole. And confusing the two, I make nullity, nihil. (pp. 80-82)

4. It should be noted, at least parenthetically, that the relationship between Tom and Lydia is precisely opposite to the surface domestic tranquillity which Conrad satirizes in *The Secret Agent,* or which Virginia Woolf describes (and perhaps upholds) in *Mrs. Dalloway.* For the Brangwens are bound together by their essential selves, and not by easy domesticity:

> He did not know her any better, any more precisely, now that he knew her altogether. . . . They did not think of each other—why should they? Only when she touched him, he knew her instantly, that she was with him, near him, that she was the gateway and the way out, that she was beyond, and that he was travelling in her through the beyond. (pp. 87-88)

5. Here is a later version of the experience, for example, as it occurs between Mellors and Constance Chatterley, in *Lady Chatterley's Lover:*

It was a night of sensual passion. . . . It was not really love. It was not voluptuousness. It was sensuality sharp and searing as fire, burning the soul to tinder.

Burning out the shames, the deepest, oldest shames, in the most secret places. . . .

In the short summer night she learnt so much. She would have thought a woman would have died of shame. Instead of which, the shame died. Shame, which is fear: the deep organic shame, the old, old physical fear which crouches in the bodily roots of us, and can only be chased away by the sensual fire, at last it was roused up and routed by the phallic hunt of the man, and she came to the very heart of the jungle of herself. She felt, now, she had come to the real bed-rock of her nature, and was essentially shameless. She was her sensual self, naked and unashamed. She felt a triumph, almost a vainglory. So that was how it was! That was life! That was how oneself really was! There was nothing left to disguise or be ashamed of. She shared her ultimate nakedness with a man, another being. . . . At the bottom of her soul, fundamentally, she had needed this phallic hunting out, she had secretly wanted it, and she had believed she would never get it. Now suddenly there it was, and a man was sharing her last and final nakedness, she was shameless.

What liars poets and everybody were! They made one think one wanted sentiment. When what one supremely wanted was this piercing, consuming, rather awful sensuality. (pp. 297-99)

What the experience does for Constance Chatterley it also does for Will and Anna Brangwen. It is a purgation process, and less the norm of love than a release to full, creative life.

6. Will Brangwen denies this deeper, impersonal second self, for example, when he lets his soul slip loose toward consummation with the Christian infinite. The experience is valid, for Lawrence, but inadequate, since it doesn't allow for the soul's fulfillment in time, in life, in conjunction with the body. Thus Lawrence substitutes creative, purposive labor in its place, and makes each form of satisfaction (spiritual and sensual) dependent on the other. For further discussion of the problem, see the final chapter.

7. Ursula's vision of malignant horses can be traced back, ultimately, to her basic fear of powerful male sensuality. Thus Lawrence describes a similar dream-image as the "symbol of some arrest or scotch in the living spontaneous psyche":

> For example, a man has a persistent passionate fear-dream about horses. He suddenly finds himself among great, physical horses which may suddenly go wild. Their great bodies surge madly around him, they rear above him, threatening to destroy him. At any minute he may be trampled down. (*Fantasia*, p. 251)

The example concerns a man, but the principle involved is still the same, for Lawrence traces the man's trouble to his fear of "the great sensual male activity" in himself, and we know that Ursula has battled and destroyed that activity, not in herself, of course, but in Skrebensky.

6.

STAR-EQUILIBRIUM

AT THE end of *Sons and Lovers* a man is born; at the end of *The Rainbow,* a woman; and in *Women in Love* a man and a woman meet and marry. Here is a simple formula, too simple perhaps to account for the complex structures of the novels at hand, yet suitable enough for the conscious attempt, on Lawrence's part, to work out the conditions of manhood, womanhood and marriage, as he experienced or understood them in his own life. Beyond doubt, Rupert Birkin in *Women in Love* is a further projection of Paul Morel in *Sons and Lovers:* he is the Lawrence-figure, that is to say, the author embodied in his own work, but objectively embodied and integral to the work, and not a mere mouthpiece like Mark Rampion, the Lawrence-figure in Aldous Huxley's *Point Counter Point.* Birkin is a man who wrestles with his own soul; like Paul Morel, he strives to understand what happens inside as well as around himself. As Lawrence explains it: "This struggle for verbal consciousness should not be left out in art. It is a very great part of life. It is not superimposition of a theory. It is the passionate struggle into conscious being."

What are the conditions of "conscious being," then, which Birkin struggles to define in *Women in Love?* For one thing, we know that he sloughs off past encumbrances, as Ursula Brangwen did before him in *The Rainbow.* In the early chapters, for example, Birkin rids himself of his former mistress, Hermione Roddice, a *Kulturträger* who moves among the foremost circles in art, society, and thought, but lacks a "robust self." Like so many Laurentian figures, Hermione depends too heavily upon one or two elements of being: will, spirit, and intellect are fused, within this woman, into a single passion for final abstract knowledge. Such knowledge means power to Hermione, power to hold all life within the scope of her conscious intellect, to toy with the passions there, to reduce them to finite particles of thought, and to reduce even Rupert Birkin to his abstract spiritual essence.[1] And it is here, with reference to Hermione's ravenous mind, that Lawrence strikes most deeply into the problem of diseased intellectualism—far more deeply, in fact, than the Faust legend will ordinarily take us. We know, for example, that Faust's lust for knowledge lies at the root of his mortal anguish—that the very *pointlessness* of his earthly life is part of the legend's truth. Nevertheless, his chief punishment comes in hell, in the after-life, so that the legend fails to illuminate the intrinsic destructivity of the knowledge-lust—it fails to show us that the mind can thwart and destroy the life within and around a man, on this earth, in its vain attempt to *command* emotional vitality; or conversely, that it can act in its proper role, as an instrument for self-fulfillment.[2]

Lawrence does reveal these truths, however, in *Women in Love:* "Of course," [cries Hermione, the Faustian heroine], "there *can* be no reason, no *excuse* for education, except the joy and beauty of knowledge in itself . . . nothing has meant so much to me in all life, as certain knowledge. . . . Yes, it is the greatest thing in life—to *know*. It is really to be happy, to be free." But Birkin, the Laurentian hero, argues that knowledge is a finite, bottled sort of attainment, and that true liberty, or spontaneity, can never be *known*, in the strictest sense of the word, but only experienced by the emotional self, and then treated with proper reverence by the mind. So he proceeds to challenge her pretense of freedom in a variety of ways. By sketching a goose, for instance, which lives from other centers than the mind, he strikes at the self-created void within his mistress. And a bit later on, by thwarting her powerful will, by attacking her belief in spiritual equality, he draws her vicious nature to the surface. Thus Hermione now tries to smash him over the head, at an opportune moment, with a ball of lapis lazuli. Given the nervous tension between the pair, given the lack of sturdy selfhood in the one and the lively separateness of the other, her blow becomes as inevitable as Birkin's strange reaction to it: for Birkin, dazed but alert, now leaves her room and heads for a nearby forest, where he strips off his clothes and moves naked among the flowers and fir-trees. He takes satisfaction there from the sting of the fir-boughs on his skin, from the smooth hardness of the birch-trunks, and from the "lovely, subtle, responsive vegetation," which literally enters into his blood, into his "living self." It is a communion scene, and admittedly a strange one; yet there are precedents for it in the works of writers like George Meredith, Samuel Butler, or (surprisingly enough) Paul Valéry, who wrote some of his finest poems "in that fertile region where giant trees grow like grass, where grass grows with incredible force and facility, and where the vigor of vegetative life is inexhaustible. My work was what it was [he adds]. But I felt my mind possessed of a vitality that today seems to me the most enviable of possessions." [3] Lawrence makes a similar observation in *Lady Chatterley's Lover:* "It needs sheer sensuality even to purify and quicken the mind." The sick mind, the plunge into the quickening bath of life: once past our initial bias, the vegetation scene in *Women in Love* acquires both meaning and dramatic impact.

Birkin continues to use the mind, however, as a means toward spontaneity; in fact, he holds that the achievement of "spontaneous being" involves an expansion and a liberation of mind, not a suppression of all consciousness: hence the young people of today have "too little" rather than too much mind; they are "imprisoned within a limited, false set of concepts." Or as Lawrence would later phrase it:

Our education from the start has *taught* us a certain range of emotions, what to feel and what not to feel, and how to feel the feelings we allow ourselves to feel. . . . This feeling only what you allow yourselves to feel at last kills all capacity for feeling, and in the higher emotional range you feel nothing at all. This has come to pass in our present century. The higher emotions are strictly dead. They have to be faked. ("A Propos of Lady Chatterley's Lover," *Sex, Literature and Censorship*, p. 96)

Thus Birkin's "passionate struggle into conscious being" becomes a problem in discovery; he must somehow replace the popular concepts of the feelings with broader, deeper notions, if only to release the "higher emotions" within himself, and within Ursula Brangwen, the girl he later marries. "The point about love," he tells Ursula, "is that we hate the word because we have vulgarised it. It ought to be prescribed, tabooed from utterance, for many years, till we get a new, better idea." The "new, better idea" is soon forthcoming: Birkin calls it "star-equilibrium," and he sets it forth in opposition to Ursula's belief that love surpasses the individual, and to Hermione's belief in spiritual and abstract communion. Such forms of love involve the loss of selfhood; they depend upon the ancient theory that men and women are but broken fragments of one whole, while Birkin insists that men and women have been singled out from an original mixture into pure individuality; accordingly, they must polarize rather than merge in love—hence star-equilibrium: "a pure balance of two single beings:—as the stars balance each other." Or as Lawrence puts it in *Aaron's Rod:*

Two eagles in mid-air, maybe, like Whitman's Dalliance of Eagles. Two eagles in mid-air, grappling, whirling, coming to their intensification of love-oneness there in mid-air. In mid-air the love consummation. But all the time each lifted on its own wings: each bearing itself up on its own wings at every moment of the mid-air love consummation. That is the splendid love-way. (p. 196)

Splendid, for Lawrence, because it preserves the sanctity of the individual soul, gives love direction and instrumental purpose, and thus keeps marriage from becoming a romantic stew-pot from which all flavor and body quickly boil away. Splendid, again, because the source of life lies beyond love, and therefore the individual soul, with its roots in that source, takes precedence over love: it "submits to the yoke and leash of love, but never forfeits its own proud individual singleness, even while it loves and yields."

Lawrence transcends mere egotism here; he perceives (as Mr. Leavis insists) that life takes place only in the individual, and that it is the business of love, marriage, religion and social endeavor to bring about fulfillment in the individual. "The central law of all organic life," he tells us elsewhere, "is that each organism is intrinsically isolate and single in itself." But "the secondary law of life" is this: that the individual can only be fulfilled through contact and communion with his fellow men and women. And of course, the most vital contact of all occurs between a man and a woman, so long as it preserves the intrinsic "otherness" of each participant. "Men live by love," writes Lawrence, "but die, or cause death, if they love too much." [4]

II

For convenience, these ideas have been presented in theoretical form. But Birkin's struggle to define them is always part of a larger and far more organic experience. Perhaps the classroom scene, between Birkin, Ursula and Hermione, will help to illustrate the point. Birkin's quickness and independence, Ursula's "lostness" and expectancy, have just been sketched in for us, briefly, in the opening chapters.

Now the two meet in Ursula's classroom as Birkin, the school-inspector, makes his rounds. It is a dark, drowsy day, there are catkins on the children's desks, and Ursula stands in front of the class, giving a final lesson on "the structure and meaning of the catkins." From the west window a shaft of light falls rich and ruddy on the children's heads, in a manner reminiscent of the opening pages of Dickens' *Hard Times*.[5] Thus, when Birkin enters the room, his face appears in the symbolic flood of light, "gleaming like fire." This startles Ursula terribly, almost to the point of faintness; but she soon recovers, and Birkin proceeds to underscore the conditions of their future conflict, and of its resolution:

"You are doing catkins?" he asked, picking up a piece of hazel from a scholar's desk in front of him. "Are they as far out as this? I hadn't noticed them this year."

He looked absorbedly at the tassel of hazel in his hand.

"The red ones too!" he said, looking at the flickers of crimson that came from the female bud.

Then he went in among the desks, to see the scholars' books. Ursula watched his intent progress. There was a stillness in his motion that hushed the activities of her heart. She seemed to be standing aside in arrested silence, watching him move in another, concentrated world. His presence was so quiet, almost like a vacancy in the corporate air.

Suddenly he lifted his face to her, and her heart quickened at the flicker of his voice.

"Give them some crayons, won't you?" he said, "so that they can make the gynaecious flowers red, and the androgynous yellow. I'd chalk them in plain, chalk in nothing else, merely the red and the yellow. Outline scarcely matters in this case. There is just the one fact to emphasize."

"I haven't any crayons," said Ursula.

"There will be some somewhere—red and yellow, that's all you want."

Ursula sent out a boy on a quest.

"It will make the books untidy," she said to Birkin, flushing deeply.

"Not very," he said. "You must mark in these things obviously. It's the fact you want to emphasize, not the subjective impression to record. What's the fact?—red little spiky stigmas of the female flower, dangling yellow male catkin, yellow pollen flying from one to the other. Make a pictorial record of the fact, as a child does when drawing a face—two eyes, one nose, mouth with teeth—so—." And he drew a figure on the blackboard. (pp. 39-40)

I have quoted Lawrence at length to bring out his ability to deliver, vividly and symbolically, a complex situation between a man and a woman. As Birkin puts it, there is just the one fact to emphasize: the male and female flowers, brightly colored and therefore singled out in their isolate loveliness, with the pollen flying between them. Quite obviously, this is a communion scene, a concrete illustration of "star-equilibrium," and Lawrence works it out with deftness and economy. Fact and symbol are one here, and in the next moment, when Hermione appears in unconventional pursuit of Birkin, the classroom situation broadens naturally into a tense quarrel on the problem of conscious knowledge and spontaneous life. With the class dismissed, Birkin begins a series of verbal assaults which prepare us for the pond-stoning scene, later on in the novel. Each argument smashes, that is, like a heavy stone into the shimmering surface consciousness which Hermione lives by; and each argument smashes, as well, at the female conceit which both of the rivals now exhibit: "The two women were jeering at him, jeering him into nothingness," thinks Birkin; and later, as he hammers away at their self-conceit—"There was silence in the room. Both women were hostile and resentful." Then Hermione interrupts him, appropriately enough, when he speaks of the need to live from other centers than the mind, and the two of them leave the classroom in mutual anger. In the meantime, Ursula has been attracted by the rich vitality which seems to emanate from Birkin's face and thighs. She switches off the light now, and sits down in the darkness alone, absorbed in thought. Then she begins to weep bitterly, "but whether from misery or joy, she never knew." The reader knows, however, that the classroom lesson has reached her heart—that "the structure and meaning of the catkins" has been brought home to her. For surely Lawrence has made a brilliant "pictorial record" here of any number of significant facts, "as a child does when drawing a face—two eyes, one nose, mouth with teeth—so—."

I am going to skip swiftly over a number of important scenes now in order to concentrate on the chapter called "Excurse," in which the struggle between Ursula and Birkin is finally resolved. It can be easily demonstrated, I think, that these intervening chapters are organized, successfully, along the same lines as the classroom scene, with the symbols welling up naturally out of an emotional situation, and giving it sharper focus: Hermione's murder weapon, for example, a hard, finite ball of lapis lazuli; or Birkin's favorite island and his proud male cat; or the drowned bodies at the Crich estate, with the girl's arms locked tightly about her "rescuer's" neck; then Birkin's pond, Ursula's angry father, and finally, Birkin's cat again, arching his back to Hermione's subtle strokes. These scenes give order and direction to the ritual tug-of-war between Birkin and Ursula, as the lovers fight, yield, or stand aloof from each other till that final burst of anger which leaves them free for consummation. I refer, of course, to the afternoon drive in Birkin's motor car, when he offers Ursula three rings and she accepts them; but a moment later she insists that he still belongs to his former mistress, Hermione, and Birkin calls her a fool for saying so; then he stops the car, and she

clambers out and lashes back at him with magnificent invective:

> Yes, I am. I *am* a fool. And thank God for it. I'm too
> big a fool to swallow your cleverness. God be praised.
> You go to your women. . . . Go to your spiritual brides—
> but don't come to me as well, because I'm not having
> any, thank you. You're not satisfied, are you? Your spir-
> itual brides can't give you what you want, they aren't
> common and fleshy enough for you, are they? So you
> come to me, and keep them in the background! You will
> marry me for daily use. But you'll keep yourself well
> provided with spiritual brides in the background. I know
> your dirty little game. . . . Then *go* to her, that's all I
> say, *go* to her, *go*. Ha, she spiritual. . . . What does she
> care for, what is her spirituality? What *is* it? . . . I tell
> you it's *dirt, dirt,* and nothing *but* dirt. . . . She wants
> petty, immediate *power,* she wants the illusion that she
> is a great woman, that is all. In her soul she's a devilish
> unbeliever, common as dirt. That's what she is at the
> bottom. And all the rest is pretence—but you love it.
> You love the sham spirituality, it's your food. And why?
> Because of the dirt underneath. Do you think I don't
> know the foulness of your sex life—and hers?—I do. And
> it's that foulness you want, you liar. Then have it, have
> it. You're such a liar. (pp. 350-51)

A passing bicycle gives Birkin a chance to reply.
He admits his own perverseness, his secret pleasure
in the whole process of spiritual self-destruction with
Hermione. "But Hermione's spiritual intimacy is no

rottener than your emotional-jealous intimacy," he counters. She throws the rings in his face and stalks off.

Birkin feels tired and weak, but relieved and, in a strangely *Dantesque* manner, purged of the last remnants of his diseased love for Hermione.[6] He wants Ursula to come back, he sits down on a bank and picks up the fallen rings as "little tokens of the reality of beauty," but he still maintains his old position:

Fusion, fusion, this horrible fusion of two beings, which every woman and most men insisted on, was it not nauseous and horrible anyhow, whether it was a fusion of the spirit or of the emotional body? Hermione saw herself as the perfect Idea, to which all men must come: And Ursula was the perfect Womb, the bath of birth, to which all men must come! And both were horrible. Why could they not remain individuals, limited by their own limits? Why this dreadful all comprehensiveness, this hateful tyranny? Why not leave the other being free, why try to absorb, or melt, or merge? One might abandon oneself utterly to the *moments*, but not to any other being. (p. 353)

A moment later Ursula drifts back and affirms his stand. "See what a flower I found you," she tells him, and this offering of the life-symbol serves as a final pledge between them: he has already brought her the rings, the bonds of love; now she brings him the flower, the confirmation of single loveliness of life, and their "freedom together" is established. Later they take tea in a private room in town, and Ursula, embracing him, finds a kind of physical confirmation of the life-source at the back and base of his loins: "And now, behold, . . . from the strange marvellous flanks and thighs, deeper, further in mystery than the phallic source, came the floods of ineffable darkness and ineffable riches." Then the chapter ends with a perfect fusion of action and symbolism, as the two children of an industrial age drive on to Sherwood forest, take each other there in "mystic love," and spend their first night together in their parked automobile, in the depths of the forest.

III

Yet if Birkin and Ursula turn towards fuller life, this is only one of the major movements of the novel. There is also the deathward affair between Gerald Crich and Gudrun Brangwen, which seems to provide symbolic contrast with "star-equilibrium." Thus Lawrence speaks of Crich as "a phase of life incarnate"; he depicts him as the perfect instrument of industrial power and applies to his development this maxim: that an individual can pass through an actual phase of civilization in his own life. The phase which Gerald passes through, fatally, is "Northern ice-destructiveness"—the destruction of civilization, that is, through the gradual mass reduction of human beings to mere instruments in the general scheme of industrial productivity. As voiced by Gerald, this scheme involves his own relentless will and intellect, on the one hand; resistant matter, on the other; and between the two, the perfect machine or system, the perfect mechanical activity which leads to the necessary and time-honored conquest of "inanimate Matter" (in this case, coal). But the scheme is not without its basic hazards: once Crich has established it, for example, he finds that he has been pursuing an abstraction, after the fashion of the young John Stuart Mill, so that a sudden spell of inactivity lays bare a strange void within himself, "as if his centres of feeling were drying up." But where Mill turned to Wordsworth's poetry for relief, Crich turns in a likelier direction, towards Gudrun Brangwen, Ursula's younger sister, who seems to offer him the promise of affective replenishment.[7]

Gudrun is a vital, aristocratic woman, an artist by profession, and Lawrence marks her out for us with a certain amount of admiration—hence Gudrun dances hypnotically before the puzzled cattle on the Crich estate; she receives a tribute of flowers, the life-symbol, from the death-driven Crich family; and, in a memorable display of pride and spirit, she snatches Birkin's letter from a mocking crowd of decadent intellectuals at the Pompadour Cafe. She is also a lovely woman, dressed always in bright colors, in handsome gowns, and her sheer sensual ap peal is delivered to us at every turn. Nevertheless, she is much more cynical, at heart, than Gerald Crich, and her woman's will is much more suitable to the struggle for personal rather than widespread social power. That struggle is focused, incidentally, in the chapter called "Rabbit," as each of the future lovers tries to subdue the stubborn rabbit Bismarck, the squirming bundle of life which young Winifred Crich values as *un mystère, ein Wunder*. But each of them is badly scratched in the process, and, as the rabbit bursts wildly around a small enclosed yard, they mock it, they show each other the deep scars on their arms, and smile obscenely, as initiates to the "abhorrent mysteries" which will surely follow. This is their bond or pledge, then, to that future violent ripping at each other's souls which ends in Gerald's death. Only the child Winifred sees the rabbit as magnificently alive: "Let its mother stroke its fur then, darling, because it is so mysterious," she says as the chapter ends.

Yet in the early stages of their affair, Gudrun's attraction to Gerald seems based upon his command of social power. Their first kiss, for example, takes place under the colliery railway bridge, where the colliers press their sweethearts to their breasts: "And now, under the bridge," thinks Gudrun, "the master of them all pressed her to himself." Later, on the continent, Gerald amazes her with his facile social charm: "*He's* a whole saturnalia in himself, once he is roused," she tells Ursula; "I shouldn't like to say whose waist his arm did not go round . . . every woman in the room was ready to surrender to him. . . . And you know, afterwards—I felt I was a whole *roomful* of women." In the end, however, Gerald's power, his potential worldly prominence, is not enough for Gudrun; she is far too proud and intelligent to accept his world, and eventually she resents his promiscuity as well, his Don Juan complex, which makes her just another formidable challenge to his will.

What Gudrun objects to, fundamentally, is the lack of "passionate purpose" in Gerald's life. And here Lawrence goes beyond the usual concept of the industrialist-as-emotional-child. He reminds us, first of all, that Crich has accidentally killed a younger brother, and that he seems antagonistic, at the subjective level, towards his fellow men, so that the mark of Cain is upon him. Then he relates this, skillfully, with the mass reduction process which Gerald has brought about in his capacity as an industrialist: to reduce one's fellow men to instruments is to destroy them. Finally, we become aware that Crich is a victim of his own system: like Skrebensky before him, he has been aroused to life through love, yet he remains unable to support himself outside a woman's orbit. Thus, on the night of his father's funeral (which forecasts his own), he slips off, dazed, and wanders through the dark countryside toward Gudrun's home; once there he steals up the back stairs, finds her room, and takes her as a child takes life-giving warmth and milk from its mother. Yet even this experience precipitates his downfall, for as Lawrence tells us later:

A strange rent had been torn in him; like a victim that is torn open and given to the heavens, so he had been torn apart and given to Gudrun. How should he close again? This wound, this strange, infinitely-sensitive open-ing· of his soul, where he was exposed, like an open flower, to all the universe . . . this was his cruelest joy. Why then should he forego it. Why should he close up and become impervious, immune, like a partial thing in a sheath, when he had broken forth, like a seed that has germinated, to issue forth in being, embracing the un-realised heavens.

He would keep the unfinished bliss of his own yearn-ing even through the torture she inflicted upon him. A strange obstinacy possessed him. He would not go away from her whatever she said or did. . . . (pp. 508-09)

As we know, this childishness in love, this terrible dependency upon Gudrun Brangwen, begins with Gerald's failure to find organic purpose in the man's world, in the very area of his supposed strength. And there is the gist of Lawrence's sharpest criticism of the industrialist, *per se:* not that he remains a child in love, but that he lacks all purposive being to be-gin with, in the world at large, and therefore *be-comes* a child in love. Like Skrebensky in *The Rain-*

bow, Crich fails to lead "on any side" into the unknown; he finds "life" only to lose it, because his life is pointless, and therein lies the poignancy of his death.

Through her alignment with Loerke, the dwarfish German artist, Gudrun Brangwen chooses still another sort of instrumentalism. Loerke presides like an evil genie over the Austrian hotel where Gerald, Gudrun, Birkin, and Ursula spend their fateful holiday, and Gudrun admires him for his complete cynicism. She shares with him, moreover, that philosophy whereby art becomes an end in itself, or interprets only the joys of instrumentality and pure motion in the industrial world. As Birkin points out, her attraction to Loerke is based upon the "subtle thrills of extreme sensation in reduction" which the little man can bring to her in love. Loerke is both homosexual and sadistic; he prefers brutal, stupid men or thin, adolescent girls as his love-partners, and this is well in keeping with his role as advance scout in the long process of Northern ice-destructiveness —"the wizard rat that swims ahead" on the sewer stream. He is an expert, then, in pure sensuous reduction and refined analysis: if Gerald can bring Gudrun the direct, violent plunge toward death, the process becomes more subtle and ecstatic with Loerke; and so Gudrun turns to him, almost hypnotically, in the final chapters.

Gerald had penetrated all the outer places of Gudrun's soul. . . . Knowing him finally she was the Alexander seeking new worlds. But there *were* no new worlds, there were no more *men*, there were only creatures, little, ultimate *creatures* like Loerke. The world was finished now, for her. There was only the inner, individual darkness, sensation within the ego, the obscene religious mystery of ultimate reduction, the mystic frictional activities of diabolic reducing down, disintegrating the vital organic body of life. . . .

Of the last series of subtleties, Gerald was not capable. He could not touch the quick of her. But where his ruder blows could not penetrate, the fine, insinuating blade of Loerke's insect-like comprehension could. At least, it was time for her now to pass over to the other, the creature, the final craftsman. . . . (pp. 515-16)

Such passages give us a good indication of what Lawrence means by Northern ice-destructiveness— the use of will, spirit, and intellect to bring about (in a variety of ways) a complete breakdown in organic life. But in *Women in Love* he also speaks of another and older form of destructiveness, the "awful African process" of sun-destruction, which seems to be based on purely physical exploitation of organic life— "knowledge arrested and ending in the senses, mystic knowledge in disintegration and dissolution." This process corresponds, essentially, to the immersion in blood-intimacy which Lawrence criticized in *The Rainbow*—and once more we see the intrinsic twofold criticism, in his novels, of the flesh as well as the spirit.[8] Thus Birkin rejects these complementary modes of dissolution (in Hermione and in Ursula) as he struggles to achieve organic being.

In the meantime, the surge towards ice-destruction continues in Gerald Crich: for if Loerke is the finer craftsman in this process, Crich is the larger, more symbolic figure. As the "omen of the universal dissolution into whiteness and snow," he must come to his death in the snow-filled mountains of the Austrian Tyrol, a victim of "frost knowledge, death by perfect cold." And so the ordeal by ice—the holiday gathering at an Austrian inn—becomes the perfect climactic arrangement for the novel. Here Birkin and Ursula burn out shame and corruption from their souls through "sensual fire"; here Gudrun sees herself, at last, as clock-faced and, by implication, clock-hearted; here too the "million wheels and cogs and axles" fly apart which once held Gerald together. And as usual, Lawrence achieves all this on both literal and symbolic levels: when the two couples first come to the Tyrol inn, for example, the mountains rise up before them and cradle between their icy slopes a great white valley, a cul-de-sac of snow and mountains which Lawrence calls "the centre, the knot, the navel of the world, where the earth belonged to the skies, pure, unapproachable, impassable." [9] And Gerald wanders straight to the heart of this knot after nearly murdering Gudrun in their final clash. His grip upon consciousness gone, he climbs blindly across the steep slopes, higher and higher, with a small bright moon shining down upon him, until he stumbles across "a half-buried Crucifix, a little Christ under a little sloping hood, at the top of a pole." Crich knows at once that someone is going to murder him, for this is the Christ of his own making, the Christ who presides over the whole world of Northern ice-destructiveness, and who symbolizes, like the bright transfixing moonlight, that form of mental-spiritual consciousness which exploits and corrupts the source of life. And perhaps he is also the Christ of *Aaron's Rod*, and other writings, who *wants* Judas to betray him, who wants to be murdered, just as Gerald wants his own throat cut in the opening chapters of *Women in Love:* "You seem to have a lurking desire to have your gizzard slit," Birkin tells him then, "and imagine every man has his knife up his sleeve for you." Birkin means here that the man who fears murder profoundly desires it, and in the chapter at hand, the Christ symbol calls up this self-created desire in Gerald's heart. And so he stumbles along, waiting for the final blow, until he reaches the hollow cradle of the pass, the knot and navel of the world, where he slips and falls and completes his own destruction: for something breaks in his soul *as he falls,* not afterwards, and it is direct knowledge of this spiritual death, preceding the physical, which Lawrence delivers, artistically, to his readers.

NOTES

1. But as Lawrence puts it in his famous essay on Poe:

To *know* a living thing is to kill it. You have to kill a thing to know it satisfactorily. For this reason, the desirous consciousness, the SPIRIT is a vampire.

One should be sufficiently intelligent and interested to know a good deal *about* any person one comes into close contact with. *About* her. Or *about* him.

But to try to *know* any living being is to try to suck the life out of that being.

Above all things, with the woman one loves. Every sacred instinct teaches one that one must leave her unknown. You know your woman darkly, in the blood. To try to *know* her mentally is to try to kill her. Beware, oh woman, of the man who wants to *find out what you are.* And, oh men, beware a thousand times more of the woman who wants to *know* you, or *get* you, what you are. . . .

Man does so horribly want to master the secret of life and of individuality *with his mind.* It is like the analysis of protoplasm. You can only analyse *dead* protoplasm, and know its constituents. It is a death process.

Keep KNOWLEDGE for the world of matter, force, and function. It has got nothing to do with being. (*Studies in Classic American Literature,* pp. 101-02)

Yet Hermione desperately wants such knowledge of Birkin's being, in *Women in Love,* to fill up the void within herself.

2. Thus, in most of the novels, Lawrence's heroes use their intellect and will in an instrumental manner, in order to determine and select the vital forms of love, and to reject the disintegrative forms. Interestingly enough, this seems to correspond with the use of will and intellect prescribed in Dante's *Purgatorio* (Canto XVIII), where Virgil holds that merit, or ethics, lies not in loving either truly or falsely, but in exercising the intellect to determine the proper forms of love, and in exercising the will in choosing to follow these forms. For the best discussion of this and other aspects of *Women in Love,* see F. R. Leavis' articles in *Scrutiny,* Autumn 1950, March 1951, June 1951. The present chapter is based, in part, upon Mr. Leavis' work.

3. *Selected Writings,* p. 154. George Meredith tells us much the same thing in *Diana of the Crossways:* "Thus does Nature restore us, by drugging the brain and making her creature confidingly animal for its new growth" (p. 364). And in *The Way of All Flesh,* Samuel Butler goes even further: his heroes visit the Zoological Gardens for "an influx of new life," and drink in especially large draughts of it from a baby elephant (see Chapter LXXIX).

4. In a sense, Lawrence takes up where Schopenhauer left off. He assumes the destructive nature of the unchecked will, and of a certain kind of cold, corrosive desire; but then he calls for the cessation of that will and desire, and in its stead, a kind of balance or polarity in love, which will allow *spontaneous* desire to well up from within and bring fulfillment. Besides this, he calls for the subordination of love to passionate, purposive action, since absolute love is inevitably destructive.

5. Dickens uses a ray of sunlight, pouring through one of the bare classroom windows, to characterize his heroine, Sissy Jupes, and the villainous Bitzer: "But, whereas the girl was so dark-eyed and dark-haired, that she seemed to receive a deeper and more lustrous colour from the sun, when it shone upon her, the boy was so light-eyed and light-haired that the self-same rays appeared to draw out of him what little colour he ever possessed" (*Hard Times*, pp. 3-4). In *The Great Tradition*, F. R. Leavis finds this passage especially Laurentian, with its "dark-vitality" and "light-sterility" equation (p. 231). One might also contrast Birkin's emphasis on the "facts" of organic life, in *Women in Love*, with Gradgrind's more utilitarian cry of "Fact, fact, fact!" in *Hard Times*. It looks strongly as if Lawrence took his cue from Dickens.

6. The whole interplay between Birkin and Ursula, in this chapter, seems to correspond with the close of Dante's *Purgatorio*, where Beatrice scolds the pilgrim for his traffic with the "Sirens." In each case, the outward scene is peaceful and sylvan, the "purgation" comes at the end of a long conflict, and most important of all, the psychological premise is the same: that it is not enough to repent and have done, in isolation from the beloved—one must also be purged in conjunction with the beloved, so that the past life is resolved *through* the present relationship, and cannot coexist with it. Thus, at the end of the *Purgatorio*, Beatrice makes the pilgrim relive his shame in relationship to her, in order to prevent all possible recurrences of the old evil; and in *Women in Love*, Ursula does the same.

7. I refer, of course, to Chapter V, "A Crisis in My Mental History," in John Stuart Mill's *Autobiography*. Mill's famous question: "Suppose that all your objects in life were realized . . . would this be a great joy and happiness to

you?"; his answer, "No!"; his sense of emptiness; the disintegration of his feelings; even his abstract goal, the "good of humanity" —all this corresponds to Crich's predicament. We know that Lawrence had read Mill (see Jessie Chambers' biography, p. 113), but whether he had specifically read the *Autobiography* remains uncertain.

8. This helps to explain why Lawrence insists, in *The Plumed Serpent*, that Quetzalcoatl is god of the two ways, of the two forms of consciousness, mental and physical, in which he believed; it also helps to explain why Lou Carrington rejects her mindless groom in *St. Mawr*, why Ursula Brangwen rejects a faun-like suitor, Anthony Schofield, in *The Rainbow*, and why the gamekeeper's intellectual and cultural background is reinforced, between versions one and three of *Lady Chatterley's Lover*. It is wholeness of being which Lawrence always emphasizes. If, at one point in his life, he poses the problem of completely physical existence, he never commits himself to a solution—while in the vast bulk of his work he decidedly upholds organic life.

9. For the conceptual origin of this passage, see *Twilight in Italy*, where Lawrence speaks of the Alps as follows:

> There, it seemed, in the glamorous snow, was the source of death, which fell down in great waves of shadow and rock, rushing to the level earth. And all the people of the mountains, on the slopes, in the valleys, seemed to live upon this great, rushing wave of death, of breaking-down, of destruction.
>
> The very pure source of breaking-down, decomposition, the very quick of cold death, is the snowy mountain-peak above. There, eternally, goes on the white foregathering of the crystals, out of the deathly cold of the heavens; this is the static nucleus where death meets life in its elementality. (pp. 280-81)

He also finds his holiday-inn at the German hotel on Lake Lugano:

And it seemed here, here in this holiday-place, was the quick of the disintegration, the dry-rot, in this dry, friable flux of people backwards and forwards on the edge of the lake, men and women from the big hotels, in evening dress, curiously sinister, and ordinary visitors, and tourists, and workmen, youths, men of the town, laughing, jeering. It was curiously and painfully sinister, almost obscene. (p. 307)

7.

NO MAN'S LAND

LAWRENCE belongs to that school of writers whose work is often more explorative, more interrogative, than affirmative.[1] His function is to ask new questions, to confront us with new values and inescapable contradictions—or in his own words, to "lead into new places the flow of our sympathetic consciousness, and [to] lead our sympathy away in recoil from things gone dead." Thus he shows us Paul Morel, at the end of *Sons and Lovers*, stepping out quickly in a new direction, away from his three discarded loves; or Ursula Brangwen, in *The Rainbow*, facing that radiant arch expectantly, her soul new-born, her old selves shed behind her like so many wrinkled skins;— and now, in *Women in Love*, he gives us Rupert Birkin, lopped and bound in a marriage which gives him peace but already pulls too tightly on his freedom to develop. Birkin is no sooner married, for example, than he begins to expound to Gerald Crich on the repulsive nature of marriage in the old sense: "It's a sort of tacit hunting in couples: the world all in couples, each couple in its own little house, watching its own little interests and stewing in its own little privacy—it's the most repulsive thing on earth." Gerald promptly agrees, and the two men search for a more expansive way of life:

"You've got to take down the love-and-marriage ideal from its pedestal. We want something broader. I believe in the *additional* perfect relationship between man and man—additional to marriage."

"I can never see how they can be the same," said Gerald.

"Not the same—but equally important, equally creative, equally sacred, if you like."

Gerald moved uneasily. "You know, I can't feel that," said he. "Surely there can never be anything as strong between man and man as sex love is between man and woman. Nature doesn't provide the basis."

"Well, of course, I think she does. And I don't think we shall ever be happy till we establish ourselves on this basis. You've got to get rid of the *exclusiveness* of married love. And you've got to admit the unadmitted love of man for man. It makes for a greater freedom for everybody, a greater power of individuality both in men and women."

"I know," said Gerald, "you believe something like that. Only I can't *feel* it, you see." He put his hand on Birkin's arm, with a sort of deprecating affection. And he smiled as if triumphantly. (p. 403)

Gerald's triumphant smile coincides, I think, with our own. We find no place, in our society, for that "unadmitted love of man for man" which Lawrence tried to project throughout his writings. And so we tend to explain the male-love theme in his works on personal or psychological grounds: hence Harry Moore examines the possibility of homosexuality, and then discards it; or he describes the wrestling bout in *Women in Love* as a form of athletic mysticism, and then suggests—"only as a possibility"— that Lawrence was merely trying to identify his personal frailness, in such chapters, with the hero's physical strength (*Life and Works*, pp. 165-66). Perhaps he was. But with one or two exceptions, the friendship scenes in other books do not involve athletics, so that argument falls through on the simple grounds of logic. As for homosexuality (which Moore discounts), the plain fact is that Lawrence was aware of it, and that he rejected it himself as mechanistic and destructive.[2]

Actually, it is a question here of values, and of emotional possibilities, rather than personal failings: we cannot "psychologize" the problem away; we have to face it in terms of the gaps and failures in modern thought itself. For if other cultures than our own have struggled with the friendship problem (the Greeks, the Elizabethans, the old Germanic tribes, the medieval knights), today we largely deny that such a problem exists. Apparently, we see a kind of no man's land between the casual and the homosexual liaison—and if Lawrence has been foolish enough to inhabit it, that is largely his affair. But let us see, at the least, how much of the forbidden ground he has explored, and with what success, if any.

II

The major expression of the brotherhood theme occurs in *Women in Love,* but a later story, "The Blind Man," may serve here as a short and simple introduction to Lawrence's position. As you may remember, the "blind man," Maurice Pervin, is caught and held within a state of blood-prescience as the story opens. He has enjoyed the rich sensual consummation with his wife, but somehow the experience has proved inadequate. Occasionally, a terrible weariness, a sense of being closed in and swamped with darkness, overwhelms them both. Isabel nearly screams with the strain; she seeks out friends for comfort, but finds them shallow and impertinent in the face of the rich, dark world she shares with her husband. Maurice too is seized with fits of depression, for at times his sensual flow is checked and thrown back, so that a kind of "shattered chaos" occurs within his blood. In the end, however, his energies are aligned and utilized through the friendship rite with Isabel's cousin, the intellectual neuter, Bertie Reid. To repeat only the crucial passage: the two men are talking together in the barn, when Pervin suddenly asks the bachelor lawyer if he may touch him; Bertie complies, and Maurice covers his face, shoulder, and arm with his sensitive fingers, and then asks him to touch his own blind eyes; again Bertie complies—

He lifted his hand, and laid the fingers on the scar, on the scarred eyes. Maurice suddenly covered them with his own hand, pressed the fingers of the other man upon his disfigured eye-sockets, trembling in every fibre, and rocking slightly, slowly, from side to side. He remained thus for a minute or more, whilst Bertie stood as if in a swoon, unconscious, imprisoned.

Then suddenly Maurice removed the hand of the other man from his brow, and stood holding it in his own.

"Oh, my God," he said, "we shall know each other now, shan't we? We shall know each other now." (*The Portable D. H. Lawrence,* p. 103)

Yet as Maurice overflows "with hot, poignant love," Bertie shrinks back, afraid for his life. And when both return to Isabel: "He could not bear it that he had been touched by the blind man, his insane reserve broken in. He was like a mollusc whose shell is broken." On the other hand, Maurice now stands before his wife, feet apart, "like a strange colossus": "We've become friends," he shouts, and though Isabel's gaze turns, painfully, on the haggard, broken lawyer, she replies, "You'll be happier now, dear." A path, a way out of the darkness has just been opened up for them, then quickly and ironically shut off by Bertie's fear of close, passionate friendship. Yet the human possibility is also clearly there: before this experience, Maurice had seemed strong-blooded and healthy to Isabel, but at the same time, cancelled out; now a new world has been revealed to him, beyond the binding intimacy of marriage and the obvious limitations of a single form of consciousness.

Clearly this is the primary function of male friendship in Lawrence's world: the step beyond marriage which makes marriage possible, the break-through to a fuller life which Lawrence tried to project, in a dozen different ways, in all his novels. This is the first important thing to remember, at any rate, when considering the friendship theme in *Women in Love*.

In the second chapter of that novel, there is a sharp quarrel between Rupert Birkin and his friend, Gerald Crich. Then the two men part with casual unconcern, and each of them suppresses his strange, burning attraction towards the other. Their friendship takes a sharp upswing, however, when Gerald's sister Diana drowns, and Birkin tries (unsuccessfully) to draw him away from the dreadful scene. In the stress of the moment, Gerald confesses that he would rather chat with Birkin than do anything else: "You mean a lot to me, Rupert, more than you know." Later, when Birkin becomes ill, Gerald does visit him, and sits indulgently by his bed, musing, as they talk, that the quick, slim man beside him seems too detached for any depth of friendship. Birkin's thoughts run on opposite lines: he suddenly sees his lifelong need "to love a man purely and fully," and so he tosses forth a first crude version of *Blutbrüderschaft:*

"You know how the old German knights used to swear a Blutbruderschaft," he said to Gerald, with quite a new happy activity in his eyes.

"Make a little wound in their arms, and rub each other's blood into the cut?" said Gerald.

"Yes—and swear to be true to each other, of one blood, all their lives. That is what we ought to do. No wounds, that is obsolete. But we ought to swear to love each other, you and I, implicitly, and perfectly, finally, without any possibility of going back on it." . . .

Birkin sought hard to express himself. But Gerald hardly listened. His face shone with a certain luminous pleasure. He was pleased. But he kept his reserve. He held himself back.

"Shall we swear to each other, one day?" said Birkin, putting out his hand towards Gerald.

Gerald just touched the extended fine, living hand, as if withheld and afraid.

"We'll leave it till I understand it better," he said, in a voice of excuse.

Birkin watched him. A little sharp disappointment, perhaps a touch of contempt came into his heart.

"Yes," he said. "You must tell me what you think, later.

You know what I mean? No sloppy emotionalism. An impersonal union that leaves one free." (p. 235)

After this conversation, the problem drops to the background and the two men go their separate ways. Crich plunges back into business and devotes his energies to the great industrial system he wants to establish; he also makes his first advances toward Ursula Brangwen's sister, Gudrun. Birkin leaves for the south of France, returns, and finally comes to closer terms with Ursula herself. But when his hasty proposal ends in fiasco, he walks furiously away from the Brangwen home, straight towards Gerald Crich at Shortlands. He finds Crich restless and irritable with his own emptiness, and therefore glad enough to see him, and, as an antidote to boredom, equally glad to learn the rudiments of jiu-jitsu. The famous wrestling scene follows, Gerald pitting his powerful mechanical strength against Birkin's more elusive and organic energies:

So the two men entwined and wrestled with each other, working nearer and nearer. Both were white and clear, but Gerald flushed smart red where he was touched, and Birkin remained white and tense. He seemed to penetrate into Gerald's more solid, more diffuse bulk, to interfuse his body through the body of the other, as if to bring it subtly into subjection, always seizing with some rapid necromantic foreknowledge every motion of the other flesh, converting and counteracting it, playing upon the limbs and trunk of Gerald like some hard wind. It was as if Birkin's whole physical intelligence interpenetrated into Gerald's body, as if his fine sublimated energy entered into the flesh of the fuller man, like some potency, casting a fine net, a prison, through the muscles into the very depths of Gerald's physical being.

So they wrestled swiftly, rapturously, intent and mindless at last, two essential white figures working into a tighter closer oneness of struggle, with a strange, octopus-like knotting and flashing of limbs in the subdued light of the room; a tense white knot of flesh gripped in silence between the walls of old brown books. Now and again came a sharp gasp of breath, or a sound like a sigh, then the rapid thudding of movement on the thickly-carpeted floor, then the strange sound of flesh escaping under flesh. Often, in the white interlaced knot of violent living being that swayed silently, there was no head to be seen, only the swift, tight limbs, the solid white backs, the physical junction of two bodies clinched into oneness. Then would appear the gleaming, ruffled head of Gerald, as the struggle changed, then for a moment the dun-coloured, shadow-like head of the other man would lift up from the conflict, the eyes wide and dreadful and sightless. (pp. 307-08)

As the two fall back exhausted, Birkin slips off toward unconsciousness, then rouses to the terrible hammer-stroke of his heart. Gerald too is dimly unconscious, but when Birkin attempts to steady himself their hands accidentally touch: "And Gerald's hand closed warm and sudden over Birkin's, they remained exhausted and breathless, the one hand clasped closely over the other." Then the two slip back to normal consciousness, and Birkin marks out the significance of their experience: "We are mentally, spiritually intimate, therefore we should be more or less physically intimate too—it is more whole"; "I think also that you are beautiful . . . and that is enjoyable too. One should enjoy what is given"; "At any rate, one feels freer and more open now—and that is what we want." This is the *Blutbrüderschaft*, then, which Birkin has been seeking, for the aim here is not sexual gratification (most critics agree on this) but the consummation of friendship.[3] The question remains, of course: just what significance does Lawrence attach to such consummation? My own interpretation follows.

First of all, we have just witnessed a spontaneous rite or ceremony between Birkin and Crich. If the terms "spontaneous" and "rite" seem contradictory, please remember that the essence of *any* religious rite is communion, contact, or rapport between the performers and their god or gods. And for Lawrence the life-flow itself is sacred, so that the flow between Birkin and Gerald becomes a religious pledge or vow, a unique and binding experience which stems quite naturally from their separate emotional predicaments and their mutual love. This same pattern recurs, incidentally, through all the rest of Lawrence's writings on the brotherhood problem, though the rites involved are never quite the same. In "The Blind Man," for example, the clasp of Reid's hands over Pervin's eyes becomes a pledge to Pervin: "We're all right together now, aren't we? . . . It's all right now, as long as we live, so far as we're concerned?" In *Sons and Lovers* the violent fight between Paul Morel and Baxter Dawes becomes a pledge or bond of friendship between them. And in *Aaron's Rod* the writer Lilly pulls the sick flutist, Aaron Sisson, off the street, cares for him in his rooms, and (when Aaron falters in his will to live) saves him with a motherly rubdown:

Quickly he uncovered the blond lower body of his patient, and began to rub the abdomen with oil, using a slow, rhythmic, circulating motion, a sort of massage. For a long time he rubbed finely and steadily, then went over the whole of the lower body, mindless, as if in a sort of incantation. He rubbed every speck of the man's lower body—the abdomen, the buttocks, the thighs and knees, down to the feet, rubbed it all warm and glowing with camphorated oil, every bit of it, chafing the toes swiftly, till he was almost exhausted. Then Aaron was covered up again, and Lilly sat down in fatigue to look at his patient.

He saw a change. The spark had come back into the sick eyes, and the faint trace of a smile, faintly luminous, into the face. Aaron was regaining himself. But Lilly said nothing. He watched his patient fall into a proper sleep. (p. 112)

Aaron recovers, of course, and the two men grope and waver toward leader-follower unison for the rest of the novel.

A similar friendship ceremony occurs in *Kangaroo,* when the writer Somers soothes the aching throat of fatherly Ben Cooley, the would-be dictator of Australia; but Somers is looking for something beyond blood brotherhood, so the friendship fails to take. That "something beyond"—the holy leader-follower compact—is firmly established between Cipriano and Ramon, the two religious leaders in *The Plumed Serpent:* for the strange sensual rite between them is not a friendship pact but an initiation into the pantheon of living gods. Let me insist, however, that each of these incidents involves a sudden radical pledge to some more than casual relationship between two men. These men do not hold wrestling bouts, or rub each other down, or ease each other's eyes and throats at periodical intervals. Instead they pledge or fail to pledge themselves in unique, significant rites, either to "life-submission" or fuller love: mental, spiritual, physical.

By physical love Lawrence means something other than homosexuality. Indeed, he makes the point, in *Fantasia of the Unconscious,* that male relations involve the upper, spiritual poles of consciousness, instead of the lower sexual poles:

> Is this new polarity, this new circuit of passion between comrades and co-workers, is this also sexual? It is a vivid circuit of polarized passion. Is it hence sex?
>
> It is not. Because what are the poles of positive connection?—the upper, busy poles. What is the dynamic contact?—a unison in spirit, in understanding, and a pure commingling in one great *work*. A mingling of the individual passion into one great *purpose*. . . . Knowing what sex is, can we call this other also sex? We cannot. . . . It is a great motion in the opposite direction. (p. 151)

This tends to explain, I think, why Pervin is attracted to an intellectual in "The Blind Man," or why Birkin likes an industrialist in *Women in Love:* for Laurentian brotherhood seems aimed, from the first, at "a unison in spirit, in understanding, and a pure commingling in one great *work*."

Yet the sensual element is also present from the first. To explain it, we must turn to the Laurentian concepts of "touch" and "warmth" in human relationships, for the two concepts are closely connected. Thus touch is an emotional, not merely a sensual experience for Lawrence; and even as a sensual experience, *per se,* touch is not necessarily sexual. Think back, in both respects, to the episode in *Sons and Lovers,* when Paul Morel falls sick and his mother sleeps with him at night: at the height of his fever

she clasps him to her breast, and the sensual contact helps to cure him.[4] The scene here is based upon
a sensual expression of love (Paul "realizes" his
mother), but not a sexual one. And the same holds
true for the sensual contacts which we have just examined, between man and man. As Mellors puts it in
Lady Chatterley's Lover, "I stand for the touch of
bodily awareness between human beings . . . and the
touch of tenderness"; as for sex, it is only "the closest
of all touch." What Mellors constructs here, in effect,
is a scale of sensuality, with physical contact between human beings as the basic experience, and
with heterosexual love at the farthest range of the
sensual scale: thus other forms of contact, between
man and man, woman and woman, or parent and
child, can also give valid expression to other, less
intimate forms of love.[5]

As we draw these various strands of thought together, the wrestling bout in *Women in Love* begins
to take on proper meaning: first of all, it functions
as part of a general step beyond marriage to some
further living relationship; second, it functions as the
spontaneous pledge to keep that relationship alive;
and third, it involves an actual physical communion,
between self and self, or soul and soul, and therefore
functions as a mutual realization of the beloved. One
can legitimately protest, of course, that the scene
at hand goes far beyond these functions, and that
Lawrence has blown it up out of all proportion to

man's actual experience—that he has overstressed, in other words, man's capacity for physical, non-sexual communion with his fellow man, and has therefore left himself exposed to honest (and dishonest) criticism. But he has only done so as part of a more general attempt to place *Blutbrüderschaft* itself upon an ideal pedestal—and even here he has incorporated his fault into the very body of his work, and has made it part of a *problem posed*, rather than a problem solved. Birkin himself, for example, is scarcely convinced of the final validity of *Blutbrüderschaft:* "I *know* I want a perfect and complete relationship with you," he tells his wife. "But beyond that. *Do* I want a real, ultimate relationship with Gerald? . . . or don't I?" This question is partially answered, I think, by the total failure of the *Blutbrüderschaft* to take hold, and by Ursula's final pointed criticism:

"Why aren't I enough?" she said. "You are enough for me. I don't want anybody else but you. Why isn't it the same with you?"

"Having you, I can live all my life without anybody else, any other sheer intimacy. But to make it complete, really happy, I wanted eternal union with a man too: another kind of love," he said.

"I don't believe it," she said. "It's an obstinacy, a theory, a perversity. . . . You can't have two kinds of love. Why should you!"

"It seems as if I can't," he said. "Yet I wanted it."

"You can't have it, because it's false, impossible," she said.

"I don't believe that," he answered.

The book ends on this stubborn note, with Birkin's brotherhood scheme exploded in fact and theory: the concept of twin loves proves ephemeral, that is, within the fictional testing vat, and Ursula's pointed question—"Why should you?"—remains unanswered. But a decided residue of truth is left over, and Birkin echoes this in his final words. If the love of man for man can never function as a perfect parallel to married love, the question still remains—how does it function? For Birkin's insistence that Gerald should have loved him—that it would have made some difference if he did—is borne out "dramatically" in the book. As Lawrence tells us, marriage would have been a hoax for Gerald, until he achieved some pure relationship with another human being: "If he pledged himself with the man he would later be able to pledge himself with the woman: not merely in legal marriage, but in absolute mystic marriage"—or star-equilibrium. And indeed, the only point in the book at which Gerald is set free, in perfect balance with another human being, occurs just after the wrestling bout with Birkin. Had the pledge between them held, Crich might have received some badly needed nurturing of the soul. Then too, his warm, vivid chats with

Birkin, taken seriously, might well have cleared away that basic mental confusion which thwarted his will to live. But Gerald had no respect for Birkin's notions: his mind was bound by convention, his will was bent toward self-annihilation, and so, as the omen of "Northern ice-destruction," he chose to break himself in the struggle with Gudrun Brangwen.

III

So the first sortie outward from the narrow circle of marriage ends in failure for Birkin—and death for Gerald Crich. But at the same time, the possibility of some kind of brotherhood is established. In the novels that follow, Lawrence reworks this possibility along wholly different lines, scrapping brotherhood *per se* for the lordship principle, and moving much more clearly into the realm of purposive (and spiritual) endeavor. Thus Lilly, the Lawrence-figure in *Aaron's Rod*, tells Aaron Sisson to find himself a leader:

"All men say, they want a leader. Then let them in their souls *submit* to some greater soul than theirs. . . . You, Aaron, you too have the need to submit. You, too, have the need livingly to yield to a more heroic soul, to give yourself. You know you have. And you know it isn't love. It is life-submission. And you know it. But you kick against the pricks. And perhaps you'd rather die than yield. And so, die you must. It is your affair."

There was a long pause. Then Aaron looked up into Lilly's face. It was dark and remote-seeming. It was like a Byzantine eikon at the moment.

"And whom shall I submit to?" he said.

"Your soul will tell you," replied the other.

The book ends on this cryptic note, but the theme is picked up and amplified in Lawrence's next novel, *Kangaroo*, as Somers, the wandering writer, specifically rejects the old ideal of brotherly affection:

All his life he had cherished a beloved ideal of friendship—David and Jonathan. And now, when true and good friends offered, he found he simply could not commit himself, even to simple friendship. The whole trend of this affection, this mingling, this intimacy, this truly beautiful love, he found his soul just set against it . . . he didn't want it, and he realised that in his innermost soul he had never wanted it.

Yet he wanted *some* living fellowship with other men; as it was he was just isolated. Maybe a living fellowship!—but not affection, not love, not comradeship. Not mates and equality and mingling. Not blood-brotherhood. None of that.

What else? He didn't know. . . . Perhaps the thing that the dark races know: that one can still feel in India: the mystery of lordship. . . . The mystery of innate, natural, sacred priority. The other mystic relationship between men, which democracy and equality try to deny and obliterate. Not any arbitrary caste or birth aristocracy. But the mystic recognition of difference and innate pri-

ority, the joy of obedience and the sacred responsibility
of authority. (pp. 120-21)

In *The Plumed Serpent* this "mystic relationship"
among men becomes one of the basic principles of a
newly-founded religious state. Lawrence tries to
project an organic society across the pages of that
novel, a society based on living contact between man
and man, and between man and God as well. The
basic faults of that society can be left for the final
chapter; at present, we are chiefly concerned with
personal relationships, and in this respect the leader-
follower idea has a certain limited validity. There
is a natural tendency towards dominance and submission, that is, in any human relationship: mar-
riages and friendships are not miniature democ-
racies, they are living and life-giving units which
require direction as well as give and take. Lawrence
did make a mistake, however, in siphoning off
friendship and lordship into separate compartments,
for without the leaven of common sympathy, "lordship" soon degenerates into sheer brutality; [6] but he
was caught up in the larger problem of man's work
with and among men, at the time, and even then he
was quick to recognize the limitations of his position. With *The Plumed Serpent* behind him, he
could write to Witter Bynner in 1928:

On the whole, I think you're right. The hero is obsolete,
and the leader of men is a back number. After all, at the

back of the hero is the militant ideal: and the militant ideal, or the ideal militant seems to me also a cold egg. . . . On the whole I agree with you, the leader-cum-follower relationship is a bore. And the new relationship will be some sort of tenderness, sensitive, between men and men and men and women, and not the one up one down, lead on I follow, *ich dien* sort of business. So you see I'm becoming a lamb at last. . . . (*Letters,* p. 719)

The tenderness theme, set forth that same year in *Lady Chatterley's Lover,* represents the third and final phase of the friendship problem. The lordship theme has been cast aside, and the brotherhood theme long since abandoned—though to be more accurate, both themes have been sharply modified, dropped to the background, and realigned within the larger scheme of the novel at hand. Now man and woman move forth refreshed from the central marriage unit, and bring the sense of touch or tenderness, which marriage has roused in them, to all their human relationships. Now Connie tells Mellors that the future depends on this gift of tenderness, and the gamekeeper replies by citing his experience as a leader of men in the first World War:

Ay . . . You're right. It's that really. It's that all the way through. I knew it with the men. I had to be in touch with them, physically, and not go back on it. I had to be bodily aware of them and a bit tender to them, even if I put 'em through hell. It's a question of awareness, as Buddha said. But even he fought shy of the bodily awareness, and that natural physical tenderness, which is the best, even between men, in a proper manly way. Makes 'em really manly, not so monkeyish. (p. 335)

"That natural physical tenderness . . . even between men, in a proper manly way." Lawrence corrects here his overemphasis on physical, non-sexual male communion in *Women in Love;* he arrives, further, at a valid mode of approach to life, at a change in being and a change, even, in the quality of human relationships; but he does not wholly solve the problem posed in *Women in Love,* because, it seems, that problem is insoluble. There must always be a certain amount of conflict between a man's friendships, however deep, and his love for his wife, since marriage is always *central* to his fulfillment, while friendships are peripheral and expendible, though paradoxically vital.[7] Yet Lawrence brings us, nonetheless, a vivid sense of this ever-present conflict: by plunging into basic human complications, by emerging, eventually, in some new direction, with new problems posed and old ones solved, exhausted, or laid aside unsolved, he broadens and deepens the scope of our own strait-jacket lives, and makes us face the full extent of our own dilemmas. For as William Blake would have it, we never know what is enough unless we know what is more than enough.

NOTES

1. As André Gide points out, Dostoievsky is another writer who poses rather than resolves some of the more difficult problems which confront him. Gide also traces part of Dostoievsky's cool reception in France to the presence of unresolved elements in his work, and cites this as a common hazard for the interrogative writer:

> The public is but ill-pacified by the author who does not come to a strikingly evident solution. In its eyes, it is the sin of uncertainty, indolence of mind, lukewarmness of convictions. And most often, having little liking for intelligence, the public gauges the strength of a conviction by naught but the violence, persistence, and uniformity of the affirmation. (*Dostoievsky*, p. 45)

2. Witness his handling of Ursula's lesbian affair in *The Rainbow*, and of Loerke's implied affairs in *Women in Love*. His objections to such unions were based, I think, on two distinct beliefs: 1) that men and women must be singled out into pure malehood and pure femalehood; and 2) that homosexual love, like oedipal love, is mechanistic and obsessive—an imposition from without, and therefore a sin against spontaneous life.

3. Harry Moore points out (not quite correctly) that "none of these scenes suggests any form of sexual gratification." He also shows that John Middleton Murry, the chief source for Gerald Crich, did not accuse Lawrence of "what is generally understood by the word homosexuality," and that other critics and biographers, friendly or hostile, generally concur on this point (*Life and Works*, pp. 165-66). Several of these critics have argued, however, that Law-

rence proffers another and more innocent brand of homosexuality, which seems to correspond with "the bisexuality of our own infant pasts" (*e.g.*, Diana Trilling, *The Portable D. H. Lawrence*, p. 22). I believe there is one genuine example of this sort of experience in Lawrence's first novel, *The White Peacock*, as George Saxton gives Cyril Beardsall a rubdown after a short swim:

> He saw that I had forgotten to continue my rubbing, and laughing he took hold of me and began to rub me briskly, as if I were a child, or rather, a woman he loved and did not fear. I left myself quite limply in his hands, and, to get a better grip of me, he put his arm round me and pressed me against him, and the sweetness of the touch of our naked bodies one against the other was superb. It satisfied in some measure the vague, indecipherable yearning of my soul; and it was the same with him. When he had rubbed me all warm, he let me go, and we looked at each other with eyes of still laughter, and our love was perfect for a moment, more perfect than any love I have known since, either for man or woman. (p. 248)

But after *The White Peacock*, Lawrence seems to understand the direction of such contacts, and he rejects them. In *The Rainbow*, for example, the affair between Ursula Brangwen and Winifred Inger begins with a kind of innocent voluptuousness, but gradually proves nauseous and degrading. Significantly enough, it also centers around a series of swimming scenes—which makes the change in Lawrence's thought seem all the more conscious and obvious.

4. For a further example of the "healing powers" of touch, take the completely impersonal scene in *The Lost Girl*, when Arthur Witham hurts his leg while working in

the organ loft. Alvina Houghton rushes up from the chapel at the sound of the accident, and examines the wound:

> She put her fingers over the bone, over his stocking, to feel if there was any fracture. Immediately her fingers were wet with blood. Then he did a curious thing. With both his hands he pressed her hand down over his wounded leg, pressed it with all his might, as if her hand were a plaster. For some moments he sat pressing her hand over his broken shin, completely oblivious, as some people are when they have had a shock and a hurt, intense on one point of consciousness only, and for the rest unconscious.
>
> Then he began to come to himself. The pain modified itself. (p. 88)

5. There is, however, an element of "sexual sympathy" in all these forms of love. The men in Lawrence's world are drawn together, for example, by a certain amount of fellow-feeling over their common mistreatment at the hands of women. As Lawrence explains it in one of the late essays:

> . . . this silent sympathy is utterly different from desire or anything rampant or lurid. . . . it is just a form of warm-heartedness and compassionateness, the most natural life-flow in the world. . . .
>
> And it is this that I want to restore into life: just the natural warm flow of common sympathy between man and man, man and woman. . . . It is the most important thing just now, this gentle physical awareness. It keeps us tender and alive at a moment when the great danger is to go brittle, hard, and in some way dead.
>
> Accept the sexual, physical being of yourself, and of every other creature. Don't be afraid of it. (*Sex, Literature, and Censorship*, pp. 66-67)

6. We see a good example of this in one of the early stories, "The Prussian Officer," as Captain Hauptmann persecutes his orderly, Schöner, to the point where Schöner murders him. Interestingly enough, Frank Amon, among others, has tried to read "psychological undertones of homosexuality" into this story (see *The Achievement of D. H. Lawrence,* ed. Hoffman and Moore, pp. 227-28). But Hauptmann is merely a fixed, rigid, inorganic creature, and what he resents in the orderly is his organic wholeness. As Lawrence tells us:

> He could not get away from the sense of the youth's person, while he was in attendance. It was like a warm flame upon the older man's tense, rigid body, that had become almost unliving, fixed. There was something so free and self-contained about him, and something in the young fellow's movement, that made the officer aware of him. And this irritated the Prussian. He did not choose to be touched into life by his servant. . . . To see the soldier's young, brown, shapely peasant's hand grasp the loaf or the wine-bottle sent a flash of hate or of anger through the elder man's blood. It was not that the youth was clumsy: it was rather the blind, instinctive sureness of movement of an unhampered young animal that irritated the officer to such a degree. (*The Portable D. H. Lawrence,* pp. 38-39)

In other words, there is nothing homosexual about this relationship; it is simply the obverse of *Blutbrüderschaft*.

7. As Lawrence puts it in a late essay:

> A woman is one bank of the river of my life, and the world is the other. Without the two shores, my life would be a marsh. It is the relationship to woman, and to my fellow-men, which makes me myself a river of life. . . .

But the relationship of man to woman is the central fact in actual human life. Next comes the relationship of man to man. And, a long way after, all the other relationships, fatherhood, motherhood, sister, brother, friend. (*Phoenix,* pp. 192-93)

part four LADY CHATTERLEY'S LOVER AND
THE MAN WHO DIED

Life is 'fulfilled' in the individual or nowhere; but without a true marital relation, which is creative in more
than the sense of producing children, there can be no
'fulfilment': that is the burden of Lawrence's art.

F. R. LEAVIS

8.

THE ASSAULT ON GOOD WILL

CLEARLY THE brotherhood theme in *Women in Love* marks Lawrence's first attempt to conceive the whole of life in terms of living relationships: Birkin's entire world, that is, would consist of his two perfect loves—with his wife Ursula, and with Gerald Crich, his friend. But such a world proved much too small for Lawrence, and so he began his famous search, across several continents, for some broader yet nonetheless organic way of life. The search ended with the creation of a religious state in *The Plumed Serpent*—an "organic" state with a highly dubious future, since Kate Leslie, the heroine of the book, could never quite convince herself that the new religion was valid. But she could convince herself of at least one thing: "that the clue to all living and to all moving-on into new living lay in the vivid blood-relation between man and woman. . . . Out of this clue . . . the whole of the new life arose. It was the quick of the whole" (p. 398).

This is the same clue, of course, which Lawrence

exploits, fully and finally, in *Lady Chatterley's Lover*. He returns here to the central theme of his work, the love ethic, and carries it to final resolution. Admittedly, there are loose ends in the novel, there are long bursts of slovenly or didactic writing; but there is also further discovery, further insight, and a basic creative triumph which most critics tend to overlook, or at best, to underestimate. In the present chapter, I hope to define and appraise that triumph.

Constance Chatterley is perhaps the most "lost" of all of Lawrence's lost girls. She is also the most modern. Previous heroines, like Alvina Houghton, Ursula Brangwen, Kate Leslie and Lou Witt, had striven to free themselves from the social order. But Connie's freedom is an established fact, a part of her modern education. Her mother, a cultivated Fabian, wants both her daughters to "fulfil themselves"; her father, an unconventional artist, lets life take its course. And so the girls are sent to Dresden, at a tender age, to find "the beautiful pure freedom" of modern womanhood. Such freedom consists, in the main, of talk with men about art, music, politics, and other intellectual matters. There is also sex, as a kind of primitive anti-climax, but the girls soon learn to reduce their men to mere phallus-bearers, mere instruments in the act of love—so that even sex can be used for greater power and freedom. Then the war breaks out, and their Dresden "education" comes to an end.

In 1917 Constance marries the future baronet, Clifford Chatterley. About six months later he is shipped home from the war, paralyzed from the hips down—forever. Yet the Chatterleys take up life together at Wragby Hall, the family seat, on deeply intimate terms. Before the injury, their love had gone beyond mere sex, which Clifford considered a casual thing, rather obsolete, and "not really necessary." Now, since Connie likes him chiefly for his clever mind, the blow to their married life seems nicely cushioned.

At this point Clifford begins to write smart, spiteful, pointless stories for the modern magazines; he gathers an intellectual circle around him, mostly men, and becomes absorbed in what Lawrence calls "the mental life." Connie joins him in this, but the postwar talk seems rooted in envy, in fathomless spite, and time rolls on at the hall in a kind of void, unmarked by any significant human contacts. Connie grows thin and restless, and inevitably she takes a lover—Michaelis, the popular dramatist, the cynical outsider whose "stray-dog" soul appeals to her compassion. Michaelis serves her, willingly enough, in love, and she gains from him a subtle, arrogant confidence in her own powers. But the man is essentially without hope, and so, when he offers her the empty prospect of marriage based on sheer "good times," she turns him down. Furious, he chides her, at an intimate moment, for her trick of holding back in the act of love, then making the expended man "hang on" until she satisfies herself: "This speech was one of the crucial blows of Connie's life. It killed something in her. . . . Her whole sexual feeling for him, or for any man, collapsed that night." Though merely reported, this unexpected collapse suggests the structural role of sexual frankness in the novel; for Michaelis strikes deep here at Connie's unassailed belief in perfect female freedom; and Lawrence himself strikes deep, through an immediate situation, at the modern concept of sex as pure sensation, as an exercise in mutual satisfaction, with each of the lovers reduced to a mere instrument for the other's pleasure, and with the woman winding up, more often than not, in full command.

In the meantime, Connie's mental life with Clifford begins to tell on her health, so the Parish nurse, Mrs. Bolton, is brought in to replace her at her husband's side. This brings the Chatterleys' "perfect intimacy" to an end, but by this time Connie doesn't mind: "The fine flower of their intimacy was to her rather like an orchid, a bulb stuck parasitic on her tree of life, and producing, to her eyes, a rather shabby flower." Of course, the shabby flower suggests that Clifford is a moral rather than a physical parasite. Like Skrebensky in *The Rainbow*, like Gerald Crich in *Women in Love*, he is unable to maintain himself—to find purpose and direction—outside a woman's orbit. As he himself tells Connie: "You are the great I-am, as far as life goes. . . . I mean, but for you I am absolutely nothing. I live for your sake and your future. I am nothing to myself." [1] And for the same reason (the pointless quality of his own existence) Clifford now lets Mrs. Bolton mother him, "as if he were a child, really as if he were a child."

Yet the warm, motherly woman also serves him as a partial life-bath; through her influence, he drops his writing and turns to the family mines, where he soon achieves remarkable success. And here, in the fullest sense of the phrase, he becomes a "phase of life incarnate"—more sharply drawn, I think, than Gerald Crich in *Women in Love,* because his crippled body and his moral failure coalesce, in a dramatic and symbolic manner, with his personal dependency on industry—the physical round of industry—for moral support. Midway through the book, for instance, Clifford moves through the woods in his motor-chair, with Connie at his side; he expounds his firm belief to her that industry comes first, that the individual scarcely matters, and that labor must accordingly be whipped into line. Then, as the chair moves on, squashing its way through the flowers, the couple comes to a downhill stretch, and Lawrence chalks out the broader implications of the scene:

And the chair began to advance slowly, joltingly down the beautiful broad riding washed over with blue encroaching hyacinths. Oh, last of all ships, through the hyacinthian shallows! Oh, pinnacle on the last wild waters, sailing on the last voyage of our civilisation! Whither, oh, weird wheeled ship, your slow course steering! Quiet and complacent, Clifford sat at the wheel of adventure: in his old black hat and tweed jacket, motionless and cautious. Oh, captain, my captain, our splendid trip is done! Not yet, though! Down-hill in the wake, came Constance in her grey dress, watching the chair jolt downwards. (p. 221)

Later, on the return trip up the slope, the chair balks and chugs to a stop among the same hyacinths. Clifford tries angrily to start it up again, but when nothing happens, he agrees to honk his horn for the keeper. Then Mellors arrives and the motor is cleared. But Clifford now insists that the chair must make the hill by itself. It stops, starts, and stops again; he refuses aid and the chair begins to slip backwards; then Connie and Mellors run to his side, and the enraged Clifford cries out, "It's obvious I'm at everybody's mercy"—which indicates his basic weakness. Instead of finding "life-responsibility" in himself, he places it on the machine, and when that fails him, his moral (not his physical) dependency is revealed. Like Gerald Crich, Clifford is weak where the world supposes him strong: he tries to sink the roots of his life into industry itself—to make the industrial round, the motor-chair, a source of moral support; and so his crippled lower body, his crippled life-responsibility, becomes symbolic of a phase of modern life.

Clifford was an emotional child, of course, before he became an industrialist; but he remains one, afterwards, because he confuses inorganic power (and its mastery) with moral strength.

Thus Clifford has no moral feet to stand on. When Connie discovers this, earlier in the book, she turns toward Mellors, the gamekeeper, whose moral strength is obvious—obvious, since Lawrence delivers it to us in concrete terms. Mellors lives by himself, for example, in a small, secluded cottage on the Chatterley estate; his separateness of self, his otherness, is an established fact, and the lapse into dialect, the edge of surliness, are merely weapons to protect it. Plainly Connie stumbles on this tough, isolate, yet somehow vulnerable self, as she delivers a message, one day, from Clifford to the keeper. She knocks at his door and, when no one answers, goes round the house toward the sounds she hears from behind it:

She turned the corner of the house and stopped. In the little yard two paces beyond her, the man was washing himself, utterly unaware. He was naked to the hips, his velveteen breeches inclining down from his slender form. And his white slim back was curved over a big bowl of soapy water, in which he ducked his head, shaking his head with a queer, quick little motion, lifting his slender white arms, and pressing the soapy water from his ears, quick, subtle as a weasel playing with water, and utterly alone. Connie backed away round the corner of the house, and hurried away to the wood. In spite of herself, she had had a shock. After all, merely a man washing himself; commonplace enough, Heaven knows!

Yet in some curious way it was a visionary experience: it had hit her in the middle of the body. She saw the clumsy breeches slipping down over the pure, delicate white loins, the bones showing a little, and the sense of aloneness, of a creature purely alone, overwhelmed her. Perfect, white, solitary nudity of a creature that lives alone, and inwardly alone. And beyond that, a certain beauty of a pure creature . . . a lambency, the warm, white flame of a single life, revealing itself in contours that one might touch: a body!

Connie had received the shock of vision in her womb, and she knew it. . . . (pp. 76-77)

This vision is reinforced, moreover, by all of Connie's past experience: the blow to her sexual pride from Michaelis, the drain on her soul from Clifford, the pointless talks at Wragby, and the general sense of life slipping past, unlived. More positively, there are the words of Tommy Dukes, the jovial army man whom Connie calls her oracle, though "chorus" might prove the better word here, since the neutral Dukes delivers all the author's fateful judgments to the intellectual group at Wragby Hall:

Real knowledge comes out of the whole corpus of the consciousness; out of your belly and your penis as much as out of your brain and mind. The mind can only analyse and rationalize. Set the mind and the reason to cock it over the rest, and all they can do is criticise, and make a deadness. I say *all* they can do. It is vastly important. My God, the world needs criticising to-day . . . criticising to death. Therefore let's live the mental life, and glory in our spite, and strip the rotten old show. But, mind you, it's like this; while you *live* your life, you are in some way an organic whole with all life. But once you start the mental life you pluck the apple. You've severed the connection between the apple and the tree: the organic connection. And if you've got nothing in your life *but* the mental life, then you yourself are a plucked apple . . . you've fallen off the tree. And then it is a logical necessity to be spiteful, just as it's a natural necessity for a plucked apple to go bad. (p. 41)

Connie recognizes her own condition here, and later, after the wash scene, she also dimly sees her future, as Dukes invokes the democracy of touch, the resurrection of the body. Even her doctor's words resound with choral significance: "You're spending your life without renewing it." And so, as Connie loosens her intimate ties with Clifford, as she draws closer to Mellors, such words sweep through her own tired consciousness: "Ye must be born again! I believe in the resurrection of the body! Except a grain of wheat fall into the earth and die, it shall by no means bring forth. When the crocus cometh forth I too will emerge and see the sun!" Thus, when the chickens hatch, down at the keeper's cottage, the fruitless woman bends over them and cries blindly, "in all the anguish of her generation's forlornness." Then she submits herself to life, to Mellors, the keeper of life, and rouses him, in turn, to love.

II

In the love scenes which follow, Lawrence tries to convey the change of being in Constance Chatterley. And since this change takes place, in part, through sexual communion, he describes the act of love directly and vividly, in all its inward sensual aspects. To label such descriptions "pornographic" is, I think, absurd: the function of pornography, its only function, is to arouse and exploit our sexual feelings by degrading them.[2] But Lawrence wants us to discover the beauty and significance of sexual love, and so he leads us, through our sympathy for Connie and Mellors, through our repulsion from Clifford, to just such a discovery. Nor can we follow him by any other verbal means: a tract on sex might command our minds, that is, but a piece of fiction can command our sympathies as well as our minds, and thereby make our discovery more whole, our knowledge more complete. As Tommy Dukes puts it, real knowledge comes out of the *whole* corpus of the human consciousness, out of the belly and phallus as much as out of the brain and mind.

Consider, in this last respect, the limited vision of our physical existence set forth by Jonathan Swift,

that early champion of pure reason. Gulliver among
the Brobdingnagians, for example, is horrified by the
sight of a gigantic human (or Brobdingnagian)
breast: "It stood prominent six foot, and could not
be less than sixteen in circumference. The nipple
was about half the bigness of my head, and the hue
both of that and the dug so varified with spots, pim-
ples, and freckles, that nothing would appear more
nauseous." In the same vein, Constance Chatterley,
watching from the ramparts of *her* mind, finds Mellors' butting haunches a bit ridiculous and farcical,
if not exactly nauseous, in the early stages of their
love:

After all, the moderns were right when they felt contempt for the performance; for it was a performance.
It was quite true, as some poets said, that the God who
created man must have had a sinister sense of humour,
creating him a reasonable being, yet forcing him to take
this ridiculous posture, and driving him with blind crav-
ing for this ridiculous performance. Even a Maupassant
found it a humiliating anti-climax. Men despised the intercourse act, and yet did it. (p. 205)

But once Connie wakes to passion, once she begins to live from other centers than the mind, then
she is at last able to see the full beauty of Mellors'
body. And so the various descriptions of love become
dramatic centers: for the act of love itself is the com-
munion-rite in this novel, and every description of it

conveys some part of the general change of being in Constance Chatterley—from the first submission to the first adoration, from ridicule to rebirth, and then the final rooting out of shame. Granted that such passages, in close succession, sometimes leave us with the very sense of choked and unresolved "blood-intimacy" which Lawrence himself deplored in *The Rainbow*. Yet they also give us a vivid and dramatic sense of Connie's transformation, and at the same time, they sweep us along to a fuller, finer, wiser vision of our physical existence—which surely represents, in itself, a basic triumph in artistic integration:

And it seemed she was like the sea, nothing but dark waves rising and heaving, heaving with a great swell, so that slowly her whole darkness was in motion, and she was ocean rolling its dark, dumb mass. Oh, and far down inside her the deeps parted and rolled asunder, in long, far-travelling billows, and ever, at the quick of her, the depths parted and rolled asunder, from the centre of soft plunging, as the plunger went deeper and deeper, touching lower . . . till suddenly, in a sort, shuddering convulsion, the quick of all her plasm was touched, she knew herself touched, the consummation was upon her, and she was gone. She was gone, she was not, and she was born: a woman. . . .

And now in her heart the queer wonder of him was awakened. A man! The strange potency of manhood upon her! Her hands strayed over him, still a little afraid.

. . . How beautiful he felt, how lovely, strong, and yet pure and delicate, such stillness of the sensitive body! . . . Her hands came timorously down his back, to the soft, smallish globes of the buttocks. . . . How was it possible, this beauty here, where she had previously only been repelled? . . . The life within life, the sheer warm, potent loveliness. . . . (pp. 208-09)

The structual value of such passages will now—I hope—seem clear. Their absence from the censored edition makes it a kind of standing shell; and if *The First Lady Chatterley* (the initial draft) seems fresher, gayer, and easier to read, it does not bring us deep, inclusive awareness of Connie's fulfillment —and the banned version, with all of its faults, does just that.[3] Only the banned version, for example, brings us the full impact of the motor-chair scene, as Connie and Mellors finally push the defeated Clifford up the hill, and Connie gives her lover a sudden secret kiss:

She looked at his smallish, short, alive hand, browned by the weather. It was the hand that caressed her. She had never even looked at it before. It seemed so still, like him, with a curious inward stillness that made her want to clutch it, as if she could not reach it. All her soul suddenly swept towards him: he was so silent, and out of reach! And he felt his limbs revive. Shoving with his left hand, he laid his right on her round white wrist, softly enfolding her wrist, with caress. And the flame of strength went down his back and his loins, reviving him.

And she bent suddenly and kissed his hand. Meanwhile the back of Clifford's head was held sleek and motionless, just in front of them. (p. 230)

This passage does not even occur in *The First Lady Chatterley*, nor can we feel its impact through the censored edition. For obviously the closeness, the flow between Mellors and Connie, and that sudden grateful kiss, are based upon their past communions. And these strengthen even the wider meaning of the passage, since "phallic tenderness" is the force, here, which moves the dead burden of industrial civilization up the hill. "It was curious," adds Lawrence, "but this bit of work together had brought them much closer than they had been before."

III

Connie wakes to passion, beauty, and human warmth through Mellors' touch, and Mellors himself returns, from lonely isolation, to life and warmhearted love. When Connie becomes pregnant, the two decide to live together on a farm, and each sets out to divorce a former mate.[4] Here the novel ends, and here we can pause to estimate its value.

Just what does Lawrence discover, finally, in *Lady Chatterley's Lover?* The answer is obviously multiple, but stated in its broadest terms, he arrives here at a deeper and clearer understanding of what a "change in being" ultimately involves. He carries his readers along, for example, to a fuller vision of physical life, as he concentrates upon the wakening of the "phallic Consciousness" in Constance Chatterley; he fortifies the surface beauty of vision with something deeper, with "warm, live beauty of contact." But more than this, he resurrects that sense of healthy reverence towards love which made his early work so promising; the old mysticism of the middle period seems largely swept away; the emphasis on love as a mystic meeting ground, as a gateway to the beyond, is now replaced by a sense of communion, by a kind of incorporated or applied mysticism, so that the experience of love is delivered, in much simpler terms, as religious in itself. And indeed, this sense of religious communion pervades *all* the sexual passages; so that to call them "naturalistic descriptions of the sex-act," with Harry Moore, or to speak, as Diana Trilling does, of the revelations of biology, is to miss the whole tenor and purpose of the reading experience.[5] Here life refreshes life, and the universe itself becomes complete as Connie rushes home, one night, from Mellors' hut, and feels the bulge and surge of surrounding trees, or the heave of the slope beside her house. This is the "greater life of the body," the connection with the religious sweep of life itself, which Lawrence also tries to evoke in *The Man Who Died*. But now his greatest stress is on the human bond, as when Connie speaks to Mellors, late in the book, about phallic tenderness:

Shall I tell you what you have that other men don't have, and that will make the future? . . .

Tell me then.

It's the courage of your own tenderness, that's what it is: like when you put your hand on my tail and say I've got a pretty tail. . . .

Ay . . . You're right. It's that really. It's that all the way through. I knew it with the men. I had to be in touch with them, physically, and not go back on it. I had to be bodily aware of them and a bit tender to them, even if I put 'em through hell. It's a question of awareness, as Buddha said. But even he fought shy of the bodily awareness, and that natural physical tenderness, which is the best, even between men; in a proper manly way. Makes 'em really manly, not so monkeyish. Ay! it's tenderness really; . . . Sex is really only touch, the closest of all touch. And it's touch we're afraid of. We're only half-conscious, and half-alive. We've got to come alive and aware. Especially the English have got to get into touch with one another, a bit delicate and a bit tender. It's our crying need. (pp. 334-35)

Thus "touch," which the modern world regards as mere sensation, is conceived here in its fullest and finest sense, as a mode of communion, as a binding and regenerative force for love, friendship, and creative labor. It flows outward, as it were, from men and women who are "quick and alive" at emotional levels of consciousness, and thereby helps to restore some of the old warmth, closeness, and togetherness, to human tasks and relationships. Touch even resolves the old dominance-submission problem in marriage, since Connie now submits to Mellors because of the warmth between them, and he yields to her, if necessary, for the same reason—though there is no real question as to who must give direction and meaning to the marriage. But more to the point, phallic love itself now functions as the fount or core of both their lives, and they move forward, renewed, enriched, and even transformed by phallic love, to the ever-present task of pushing Clifford up the hill. They are fully alive now, and as Lawrence puts it in *Apocalypse*—

For man, the vast marvel is to be alive. For man, as for flower and beast and bird, the supreme triumph is to be most vividly, most perfectly alive. Whatever the unborn and the dead may know, they cannot know the beauty, the marvel of being alive in the flesh. The dead may look after the afterwards. But the magnificent here and now of life in the flesh is ours, and ours alone, and ours only for a time. . . . (pp. 199-200)

From this point of view, it seems unfair to call *Lady Chatterley's Lover* a *cul-de-sac*, or to say, with Father Tiverton, "that the little boat on which he [Lawrence] sails this novel will not bear the weight of the world's future which is to be its cargo." To be correct, Tiverton should speak of millions of sturdy little boats, upon uncharted seas, since Lawrence projects no social program here, but a change in the mode, condition, or quality of individual being. To "make the future," he would rouse us all to life—to individual life. Admittedly, this does not solve the *problems* of the future, but it does make them worth solving. Think back, in this respect, to *Women in Love*, where Lawrence is much less bothered by the death of Gerald Crich than by the fact that Gerald— that omen of Northern "ice-destructive" civilization —has never really lived.

IV

Clearly, then, this novel must be read as a call to individual regeneration. Yet to give Father Tiverton his due, the struggle between mind, spirit, and phallus does have social implications for the future. For the moral *precedence* of phallic marriage is firmly established as the novel ends; or to use a more relevant term, this precedence is "discovered" as Lawrence works out the problem of Clifford Chatterley's paralysis.

A number of writers have complained, however, about the symbolic nature of the paralysis. Crippling Clifford weakens the story, they have argued; he should have been left whole and potent, yet essentially sexless; then the irony would be far greater, with the potent man emotionally impotent. But this is to assume that Lawrence wrote his stories to suit his symbols, when actually he always dealt with specific situations which lent themselves, in turn, to symbolic treatment. Thus Clifford's paralysis was chiefly a dramatic fact, for Lawrence, a specific condition with at least three concrete and immediate aspects. For one thing, it served to isolate the sensual basis of human existence, and in this respect it seems roughly similar to situations in less famous works, like the play, *David*, where the aging Saul has lost the godly "blitheness" of his body:

Not because I am old [he cries]. And were I ancient as Samuel is, I could still have the alertness of God in me, and the blithe bearing of the living God upon me. I have lost the best. I had it, and have let it go. (Scene VII)

Here Lawrence holds the ancient king responsible for his lack of sensual (rather than sexual) vitality. And in *Lady Chatterley's Lover*, Connie actually holds Clifford responsible—morally responsible—for his own cold-bloodedness:

Deep inside herself, a sense of injustice, of being defrauded, began to burn in Connie. . . . Poor Clifford, he was not to blame. His was the greater misfortune. It was all part of the general catastrophe.

And yet was he not in a way to blame? This lack of warmth, this lack of the simple, warm, physical contact, was he not to blame for that? He was never really warm, nor even kind, only thoughtful, considerate, in a well-bred, cold sort of way! But never warm as a man can be warm to a woman, as even Connie's father could be warm to her, with the warmth of a man who did himself well, and intended to, but who still could comfort a woman with a bit of his masculine glow. (pp. 82-83)

Thus Clifford's impotence here is *sensual* rather than sexual; he fails to affirm the common sensual basis of human sympathy, and his paralysis helps to isolate and define his moral lapse.[6] But as we have already seen, it also helps to define a second concrete and dramatic fact: his lack of life-responsibility. Throw this "crippling" element out, leave Clifford whole and potent, and you must also toss out Mrs. Bolton, the motor-chair scene, and the sharp moral contrast with Mellors—in short, the present moral core of the novel, and much of the most successful ritual drama. For it is only through the fiasco with the motor-chair, remember, that Connie is finally purged of the deadly attachment to her husband: "And it was strange, how free and full of life it made her feel, to hate him and to admit it fully to herself. —'Now I've hated him, I shall never be able to go on living with him,' came the thought into her mind."

This feeling of freedom-through-hate brings out the final significance of Clifford's paralysis, and leads us to that aspect of the book which no one, to my knowledge, has yet examined. I refer to the whole weight of bourgeois sentiment, which represents, ultimately, Clifford's only moral asset. Our first re-

action to the word "cripple," for example, runs something like this—pity, sympathy, good will, kindness,
charity. As the novel begins, Clifford commands all
these ready sentiments; by the time it ends he commands only these sentiments—his humanity depends,
that is, not on his own worth, but upon our pity,
sympathy, and good will. And so we actually come
to hate Clifford as Connie hates him, consciously and
vividly, because he makes a false demand upon our
sympathies, because he lacks the moral strength and
human warmth which alone command our respect
and love. True enough, when Connie leaves him, she
sins against bourgeois morality—but Clifford sins
against organic life. Two moral systems clash, and
yet we recognize at once that phallic marriage is
creative and moral, above and beyond our vision of
Clifford's plight. Indeed, good will turns counterfeit
before our very eyes, because it rests on counterfeit
emotion, on easy public righteousness. Lawrence
himself had often suffered, both as a writer and a
man, from the consequences of this false morality.
Significantly enough, he had taken his own wife
away from a husband and three children, and perhaps he found an "objective correlative," in Clifford's
paralyzed state, for that whole early predicament.
Whatever the case, he knew that life had to be established, first and foremost, on an organic basis,
since the old morality could only foster deadness. As
Connie puts it:

All the great words . . . were cancelled for her generation: love, joy, happiness, home, mother, father, husband,
all these great, dynamic words were half dead now, and
dying from day to day. Home was a place you lived in,
love was a thing you didn't fool yourself about, joy was
a word you applied to a good Charleston, happiness was
a term of hypocrisy used to bluff other people, a father
was an individual who enjoyed his own existence, a
husband was a man you lived with and kept going in
spirits. As for sex, the last of the great words, it was just
a cocktail term for an excitement that bucked you up for
awhile, then left you more raggy than ever. Frayed! It
was as if the very material you were made of was cheap
stuff, and was fraying out to nothing. (p. 71)

But Connie pushes this deadness aside by reject-
ing Clifford—a physically helpless man—as her husband. And therefore she asserts the priority of phallic marriage over the old half-dead morality; and at
the same time, she also asserts what I would call the
root-value of Lawrence's work, from a social point of
view: for the new "life-morality" now acts as the
base, or better still, the fount from which the old
morality of ideals can be regenerated; it comes *before* good and evil, as we know them, and makes
them once more possible—and in this it differs radi-
cally from its supposed counterpart, Nietzsche's "mas-
ter-morality," which lies beyond good and evil.

Always, in all his books, Lawrence had tried to
show that the relations between men and women,

even between men and men, are actual, emotional, and dynamic, and not ideal, not purely mental-spiritual, and certainly not static or *status-quo*. In *The Fox* and *The Plumed Serpent* he had overstepped himself quite badly; he had sanctioned murder in defense of the life-morality: but in *Lady Chatterley's Lover* he had finally found a legitimately cruel and dramatic way to assault good will—rootless, pointless, sterile good will, or doing the "right thing" for the sake of doing the right thing. A novelist like Henry James, for instance, would have sent poor Connie back to Clifford; he would have replaced the claims of life with a rootless (if heroic) ideal. Thus Isabel Archer, Lambert Strether, Milly Theale—all of them live in accord with such ideals, at novel's end; or better still, all of them die in accord with such ideals, since no one really lives by them.[7] Now Lawrence seems to reject this kind of sacrifice as pointless; he seems to suggest that all the old ideals—love, home, husband, wife, good and evil itself—can have no vivid meaning, so long as men and women sin against life itself—the truly modern sin—and rip and tear at each other's souls at every turn. And so, he might add, we must regenerate our *selves*, we must think and feel with the whole of our being, we must resurrect the body, if we would bring the great words back to life again. For the "great words" never stand by themselves, in Lawrence's world, but always spring from living relationships, and lead to the soul's fulfillment in this life. Mellors' "chastity" or fidelity, at the end of the novel, is a case in point—not a stringent imperative, but "the peace that comes of loving."

NOTES

1. The same situation occurs, incidentally, in "The Border Line," as Philip Farquhar (John Middleton Murry?) speaks to his wife, Katherine: "I'm not real! I'm *not!*—not when I'm alone. But when I'm with you I'm the most real man alive. I know it!" But Katherine simply feels "a cruel derision of the whimpering little beast who claimed reality only through a woman." And Lawrence makes the same point in *Lady Chatterley's Lover:* "What man in his senses would put this ghastly burden of life-responsibility upon a woman, and leave her there in the void?" Clearly this is one of the most persistent themes in all his fiction, this emphasis on "life-responsibility." For the best definition of it, see *The White Peacock*, where Lettie Tempest decides "to abandon the charge of herself to serve her children":

> Having reached that point in a woman's career when most, perhaps all, of the things in life seemed worthless and insipid, she had determined to put up with it, to ignore her own self, to empty her own potentialities into the vessel of another or others, and to live her life at second hand. This peculiar abnegation of self is the resource of a woman for the escaping of the responsibilities of her own development. Like a nun, she puts over her living face a veil, as a sign that the woman no longer

exists for herself: she is the servant of God, of some man, of her children, or maybe of some cause. As a servant, she is no longer responsible for herself, which would make her terrified and lonely. Service is light and easy. To be responsible for the good progress of one's life is terrifying. It is the most insufferable form of loneliness, and the heaviest of responsibilities. (pp. 316-17)

2. Thus, as Lawrence defines it:

Pornography is the attempt to insult sex, to do dirt on it. This is unpardonable. Take the very lowest instance, the picture post-card sold under hand, by the under-world, in most cities. What I have seen of them have been of an ugliness to make you cry. The insult to the human body, the insult to a vital human relationship! Ugly and cheap they make the human nudity, ugly and degraded they make the sexual act, trivial and cheap and nasty. (*The Portable D. H. Lawrence*, p. 653)

With this definition in mind, the case for removing the ban on *Lady Chatterley's Lover* seems very strong. As Harry Moore suggests, "the time is overdue for an American publisher to make a fight for *Lady Chatterley's Lover* such as the one made . . . for Joyce's *Ulysses*." He fears, however, that the doctrinal side of the book might be considered dangerous, from a legal point of view: "Joyce merely represented; Lawrence preached" (*Life and Works*, pp. 266-67). Yet even so, he did not preach pornography or promiscuity, and so the legal fight might well be won. Certainly it seems worth the effort; it would make the book available, for the first time, to a wider group of serious readers, and though the larger American audience might take the book as pure sensation, this would scarcely harm them. In Lawrence's words:

There's nothing wrong with sexual feelings in themselves, so long as they are straightforward and not sneaking or sly. The right sort of sex stimulus is invaluable to human daily life. Without it the world grows grey. I would give everybody the gay Renaissance stories to read, they would help to shake off a lot of grey self-importance, which is our modern civilized disease. (*Portable*, p. 653)

3. In her introduction to *The First Lady Chatterley*, Esther Forbes makes out a good case for the first draft as the more human book, with regard to plot and characterization. And indeed, one might also call it a better written book, on a simple line-for-line basis. Yet the final version is much more ambitious than the original, and its achievement seems more significant—so that Miss Forbes' arguments remain unconvincing, a bit romantic, and sometimes merely prudish. The first version is a good book in its own right: that, it seems to me, is the chief argument for reading it.

4. Mellors, of course, has been separated for some time from his first wife, the terrible Bertha Coutts, who liked to "grind her own coffee" in the act of love. He now divorces her. His coming child by Connie is clearly labeled, incidentally, as "the future," and this completes the pattern I have noted in previous novels: the birth of a man in *Sons and Lovers;* the birth of a woman in *The Rainbow;* the marriage of a "man" and "woman" in *Women in Love;*—and now, in *Lady Chatterley's Lover*, with the conditions for creative love more firmly established, there is *procreative* love. This pattern is scarcely accidental, or at least not wholly so, since each of these stages represents an actual phase of development in Lawrence's thought. Indeed, he becomes almost beatific in *The Man Who Died:* he accepts the impregnation of "Isis" without qualms.

5. I am objecting here to the *terms* used by both writers; at other points in their work, Mr. Moore and Mrs. Trilling show warm appreciation of this aspect of the novel, and their arguments have actually helped me considerably.

6. In "Daughters of the Vicar," one of Clifford Chatterley's forerunners, the midget Reverend Mr. Massy, is actually potent, sexually, but he lacks the full range of human feelings, and lives chiefly from his strong, philosophical mind. Thus his dwarfish figure helps to define his lack of human sympathy, so that Lawrence can call the lofty, spiritual girl who marries him "degraded in the body," or flawed and incomplete. Compare Lawrence's attitude here with Rostand's hypocrisy in *Cyrano de Bergerac:* though Roxane is presented largely as an enticing sexual object, the long-nosed Cyrano wins her on completely spiritual grounds. Like so many sentimentalists, Rostand sees sensual beauty through the eyes and mind, rather than through the flesh and feelings. Consequently, he tries to reject the human body, in the final act, by converting his heroine into a nun. But he uses the split between mind and body *dramatically,* and this is how Lawrence uses it in *Lady Chatterley's Lover* and "Daughters of the Vicar." Unlike Rostand, however, Lawrence stresses the need to reassert organic wholeness in the face of physical shortcomings:

> Man is like this [he writes]. He has various levels of consciousness. When he is broken, killed at one level of consciousness, his very death leaves him on a higher level. And this is the soul in its entirety, being conscious, super-conscious, far beyond mentality. It hardly needs eyes or ears. It is clairvoyant and clair-audient. And man's divinity, and his ultimate power, is in this super-consciousness of the whole soul. (*The Boy in the Bush,* p. 177)

7. James would have seen through Clifford, as he saw through Gilbert Osmond in *The Portrait of a Lady;* and of course he would have pitched his story well above the level of bourgeois sentiment. But the fact remains that many of his protagonists live in accord with noble sentiments or ideals, which Lawrence would have found quite baseless (and quite destructive) as *dominant* modes of life. See especially *Fantasia of the Unconscious*, pp. 192-93.

THE FINAL VISION

As THE PROPHET of individual regeneration, Lawrence had achieved a good measure of success; his vision of love, friendship, and life-responsibility had broadened and deepened, through the major novels, and had reached its fullest scope with *Lady Chatterley's Lover*. But as a social prophet Lawrence had obviously failed; he admitted as much himself, and all his critics, past and present, have at least agreed on this one point. I suggest with some timidity, therefore, that his final vision of society is essentially sound, and I refer here not to the religious state in *The Plumed Serpent*, but to the symbolic pattern of *The Man Who Died*, and to the social content of pamphlets, letters and reviews from the last years of his life. For significantly enough, "the later D. H. Lawrence" turns from paganism *per se* to the pagan element in Christianity itself. Thus Father Tiverton feels that "Lawrence can teach Christians lessons they should have known but have forgotten"; and in my own opinion, he can teach us all, Christian or not, a vital lesson in social regeneration.

This lesson begins in 1922, when Lawrence first roughed out an interdependent social scheme in *Fantasia of the Unconscious:* the night, he said, was the time for love, and day was the time for labor— but neither form of fulfillment was exclusive of the other:

Assert sex as the predominant fulfillment, and you get the collapse of living purpose in man. . . . Assert *purposiveness* as the one supreme and pure activity of life, and you drift into barren sterility, like our business life of to-day, and our political life. . . . And so there you are. You have got to base your great purposive activity upon the intense sexual fulfillment of all your individuals. That was how Egypt endured. But you have got to keep your sexual fulfillment even then subordinate, just subordinate to the great passion of purpose: subordinate by a hair's breadth only: but still, by that hair's breadth, subordinate. (pp. 155-56)

Perhaps all studies of Lawrence should begin with this quotation, to counteract the popular distortions of his views. The surprising predominance of purpose over sex, the interdependence of love and labor— these things deserve to be underlined as constant factors in all his work. We tend to forget, I think, that Lawrence finds "the first motive for all human activity" in man's intense desire to "make something wonderful" beyond himself; we forget that sex is

never an end in itself, for Lawrence, but always a regenerative force, a mode of resurrection and renewal. The question remains, of course, renewal for
what?—a question, incidentally, which Lawrence
could never wholly answer in his books, though he
never ceased to ask it. As Mellors puts it to Connie:

Living is moving and moving on. . . . And I've no business to take a woman into my life, unless my life does
something and gets somewhere, inwardly at least, to
keep us both fresh. A man must offer a woman some
meaning in his life, if it's going to be an isolated life,
and if she's a genuine woman. I can't just be your male
concubine. (*Lady Chatterley's Lover*, p. 333)

Unfortunately, this problem of meaning is never
fully broached in the novel. There is touch, or tenderness, of course, which provides the mode for
friendship and for the collective tasks of men; but
the tasks themselves are only vaguely described, and
creative labor is mainly a personal problem, for Mellors, as the novel ends.[1] Apparently, Lawrence had
gone as far as he could go in *Lady Chatterley's Lover*,
and Father Tiverton's cry—a *cul-de-sac!*—rings still
more loudly in our ears.

The cry is not uncommon, but a change of being,
a mode of awareness, a fount for the regeneration of
old ideals—all this should be enough for one novel.
For clear-cut social patterns, we must read *The Man
Who Died* in conjunction with the Chatterley book,

and only then pass judgment on the "social prophet." I propose to follow that course in the present chapter, with a look first at *The Plumed Serpent* and other relevant works.

II

One must insist, at the outset, that *The Plumed Serpent* is not a fascist novel: for the state which Lawrence devises here is based upon *living* relationships, and upon the fundamental dignity—the organic unity—of each of its members. "We are lords among men, not lords of men," say the two religious leaders in the novel; their goal is the fusion of man's spirit and blood into new and vital unison—a universal goal which hardly jibes with Nazi racial theory. In effect, Lawrence was asserting his old claim, that the flesh is quite as holy as the spirit, and that fusion of the two, on a religious "meeting-ground," will bring out the "god-power" in man. This too is a far cry from fascism, though it is, in fact, only the other side of the emotional coin—the positive side. Hence Lawrence would later speak, in *Apocalypse*, of the great green and red dragons of the emotions: the green dragon was the great vivifier, the life-bringer and the life-maker, whom the Chinese celebrate and the Hindus see as coiling "quiescent at the base of the spine of a man"; but the red dragon was evil and destructive, "the great 'potency' of the cosmos in its hostile and destructive activity." Both dragons appear, of course, in *The Plumed Serpent,* but Lawrence has wisely combined them into a single serpent, Huitzilopochtli, whose colors vary with his function—red when militant, green when fertile and creative. But the red or militant power is now designed to *protect* creative life, rather than destroy it. As Lawrence puts it in an earlier book:

If I were dictator . . . I should have judges with sensitive, living hearts: not abstract intellects. And because the instinctive heart recognised a man as evil, I would have that man destroyed. Quickly. Because good warm life is now in danger. (*Sea and Sardinia,* p. 27)

Here Lawrence seems to confuse legitimate personal hatred with illegitimate social action. But at least his *aims* are clear, and there is no real point in confusing them with fascist aims. Indeed, his sin is one of omission rather than commission: he does not work for evil ends, either here or in *The Plumed Serpent;* he simply fails to provide an effective check against them, in the hearts of his own "judges." [2]

This is a grievous fault, but it tells us more about Lawrence than about fascism: in other words, his sin of omission points to an even greater flaw in his thinking—his naïve romanticization of society itself. For at this stage of his work, he seems to lack that brand of social wisdom which is evidenced, say, in Melville's *Billy Budd;* he fails to recognize the need

to work with institutions, even at the cost of occasional injustice. Instead he tries to base his fictional societies on living, spontaneous relationships
between man and man—but without allowing for the
complex motivations, the conflict of ideals, and inevitable rigid institutions which real collective action entails. There are no ideals, for example, in *The
Plumed Serpent,* beyond the "militant ideal" which
Lawrence himself would later dismiss as a "cold
egg." Nor are there social goals in the novel: there
is only static vitalism, or vivid and sustaining contact with the cosmos; and the religious state itself
has no direction, no collective purpose, beyond this
vital contact.[3] Thus, if Lawrence speaks of the
plumed serpent, Quetzalcoatl, as god of the *two*
ways—blood and spirit, earth and sky, dark and day-
light—he manifestly neglects the "second way": he
makes no provision, that is, for the mental-spiritual
consciousness, which remains singularly "un-fused"
in the course of the novel, just as heroine Kate Leslie, the modern mentally-conscious woman, remains
un-fused as the book ends, with respect to the new
religion.

It seems apparent, then, that Lawrence was faced
here with the same impasse which occurs in all his
work. To be sure, his own impressive critique of the
tyranny of ideals, and of the smothering rigidity of
most modern institutions, did not *exclude* such areas
of experience from his mind; but given his initial

bias, he was never able to formulate his own ideals, nor could he project a workable set of institutions for the future. In *Kangaroo,* for example, he had rejected democratic, communistic, and paternalistic states for the type of religious community he would later establish in *The Plumed Serpent.* But still later he rejected *The Plumed Serpent,* and admittedly this left him without a society, or even a set of ideals, to call his own. Yet it did not leave him in a *cul-de-sac,* since there still remained one final possibility: the merging of his own discoveries with the larger pattern of Western civilization—a merger which he first began to explore in a little pamphlet called *A Propos of Lady Chatterley's Lover.*

In this excellent postscript to the novel, Lawrence hammered away at the wisdom of the old Christian Church, and thereby implied the virtual re-paganization, or regeneration, of modern Christianity. The Church, he said, had originally been established on the first element of union in mankind, the marriage-tie; indeed, marriage was "Christianity's great contribution to the [social] life of man," and the Church in its wisdom had made a sacrament of marriage, and had provided thereby for earthly fulfillment, for "the complex development of the man's soul and the woman's soul in unison, throughout a life-time":

The Church established marriage for life, for the fulfilment of the soul's living life, not postponing it till the after-death.

The old Church knew that life is here our portion, to be lived, to be lived in fulfilment. . . . The rhythm of life itself was preserved by the Church, hour by hour, day by day, season by season, year by year, epoch by epoch, down among the people. . . . We feel it, in the south, in the country, when we hear the jangle of the bells at dawn, at noon, at sunset, marking the hours with the sound of mass or prayers. . . . We feel it in the festivals, the processions, Christmas, the Three Kings, Easter, Pentecost, St. John's Day, All Saints, All Souls. . . . And it is the inward rhythm of man and woman, too. . . . And men experience the great rhythm of emotion man-wise, women experience it women-wise, and in the unison of men and women it is complete. (*Sex, Literature and Censorship*, p. 108)

This rhythmic pattern fascinated Lawrence, and in the last years of his life, it helped to lead him toward the Christian type of society, founded upon the autonomy of the family within the state, as opposed to the various societies in which the family, or the individual, was more or less directly under state control. But the important thing to note, here, is the link which Lawrence made between phallic love and the Christian marriage sacrament:

The great saints only live, even Jesus only lives to add a new fulfilment and a new beauty to the permanent sacrament of marriage.

But—and this *but* crashes through our heart like a bullet—marriage is no marriage that is not basically and permanently phallic. . . . (p. 110)

There follows a long passage on sexual communion as the greatest of all religious mysteries, on the phallus as the connecting-link between two life-streams, and on oneness in love as the completion of the universe and the fount of life itself: "From it all things human spring, children and beauty and well-made things; all the true creations of humanity. . . ."

And here, as the basic element of union in mankind, phallic marriage finds its proper social significance. For like any good sociologist, Lawrence believed that a healthy society was founded upon the strength of the family unit—the same unit he had tried to re-define in almost all his books, but especially in *Lady Chatterley's Lover*. Now the old Church gave him a solid social basis for that unit: the rhythm of day and night, marked by the bells; the rhythm of the seasons, marked by semi-pagan ritual; and the rites of passage of life itself—all these provided Lawrence with a convenient framework for his beliefs, and he speaks in this pamphlet of the love-labor pattern of night and day, of the sexual rhythm of the year, and of the harmony, the togetherness, the fulfillment of permanent phallic marriage, "set again in relationship to the rhythmic cosmos." This constitutes, of course, a paganization or transvaluation of current Christian belief, but that is precisely what Lawrence intended, as the last thing he ever wrote attests:

The Catholic Church . . . is a great institution, and we
all like to feel romantic about it. But the Catholic Church
needs to be born again, quite as badly as the Protestant.
I cannot feel there is much more belief in God in Naples
or Barcelona, than there is in Liverpool or Leeds. Yet
they are truly Catholic cities. No, the Catholic Church
has fallen into the same disaster as the Protestant: of
preaching a *moral* God, instead of Almighty God, the
God of strength and glory and might and wisdom: a
"good" God, instead of a vital and magnificent God. And
we no longer any of us *really* believe in an exclusively
"good" God. The Catholic Church in the cities is as dead
as the Protestant Church. Only in the country, among
peasants, where the old ritual of the seasons lives on in
its beauty, is there still some living, instinctive "faith"
in the God of life. (*Phoenix*, p. 396)

The question remains, how tenable is this approach to Christianity? A Christian writer like
Thomas Greene rests comfortably in the belief that
Lawrence "never made palpable contact with the
supernatural"; he sees Lawrence as the quixotic hero
in pathetic, ridiculous, and often dishonest quest of
non-existent gods (*Sewanee Review*, Autumn 1951).
But Father Tiverton does far more justice to the
problem in *D. H. Lawrence and Human Existence*.
He praises Lawrence for his sense of "the ISness
rather than the OUGHTness of religion" (p. 124),
and calls our attention to the essential correspond-
ence between Laurentian belief and three of the cen-

tral tenets of the Christian faith: where Lawrence sees the body as a central point of man's connectedness with man, "the Christian doctrine of creation would imply the same" (p. 136); where Lawrence emphasizes the religious and spontaneous nature of sexual love, "this surely coincides with the Christian view, according to which the physical is to be taken, wholly, gratefully, and offered to God in the very act" (p. 81)—and to support this argument he even cites the Christian existentialists, "who believe that communion *is* possible" (p. 137); finally, where Lawrence argues that the Church must stress Christ Risen in the flesh, glad and whole, above and beyond Christ crucified, Tiverton cites the doctrine of the Resurrection of the Body (p. 115). Thus, on at least three counts—creation, the marriage sacrament, and Christ's resurrection—"Lawrence can teach Christians lessons they should have known but have forgotten" (p. x).

If Tiverton is correct, then the pagan element in Christianity is much stronger than most of its adherents would admit. For there seems to be room in the Christian metaphysic for the "primitive indefinite" which Lawrence always tries to evoke. Yet Father Tiverton himself has missed this point: he speaks, for example, of the conflict in Lawrence's thought between pantheism and the transcendent, Almighty God of Life; and he quotes M. Gustave Thibon on the "levelling kind of monism" which pantheism involves, the dilution of God into the world and the loss thereby of "the authentic divine imprint in things" (p. 126). But Lawrence always distinguishes between the quick and the dead, the God-stuff and the merely finite aspects of existence; and so his "pantheism" is never monistic: it is the flow of the life-force, and the connection with God comes when the human soul transcends mere finite existence and becomes one with the primitive indefinite—either through love (the sensual consummation), or through its opposite, creative labor. Thus Lawrence's "pantheism" is always transcendent, if wholeness of being is seen as perfect conjunction with the God of Life. But this is not precisely the same thing as Christian transcendence, though it seems remarkably similar to those Christian doctrines which emphasize the potential sacredness of flesh and blood, and the religious nature of man's earthly work.[4]

Perhaps these similarities and differences will be clarified if we concentrate upon the sex-experience. Father Tiverton tells us that the physical is "to be taken, wholly, gratefully, and offered to God in the very act." But Lawrence did not see sex as an *offering* to God; he saw it instead as a religious communion, an inclusive expression of the force of life itself, which nourishes and renews the true self, the second ego, the individual soul of each of the lovers. That is why he speaks of the blood as "the substance of the soul, and of the deepest consciousness," in *A Propos of Lady Chatterley's Lover;* and that is why he speaks of the "godly vitality" which comes from phallic love: for that vitality is the result of blood-contact (or "pantheistic" flux) and the soul's transcendence of merely finite being—and there is the essential difference between Lawrence's view of love and Tiverton's offer-concept. Yet the difference is not ineradicable, or at least not overly important: whether man receives the sacred flow of life which God has given him, and remains thankful for that, or whether man transcends his finite self, to participate in the God-stuff, the ultimate effect is the same: "God is the God of life, and man is free, he is not a behaviourist, he must act 'with the blood,' but it will be he who is acting" (p. 119). The words are Father Tiverton's, they are about Lawrence, but they apply to either writer's beliefs.

So Lawrence is almost a Christian, after all. But Christian or not, his use of the Christian framework gives him, at long last, a social basis for the regeneration of all the old "half-dead" ideals which Constance Chatterley reviews in *Lady Chatterley's Lover.* Thus Lawrence makes a close connection, in his postscript to that novel, between these same ideals and the "higher emotions":

And by higher emotions we mean love in all its manifestations, from genuine desire to tender love, love of our fellowmen, and love of God: we mean love, joy, delight, hope, true indignant anger, passionate sense of justice and injustice, truth and untruth, honour and dishonour, and real belief in *anything*: for belief is a profound emotion that has the mind's connivance. (*Sex, Literature and Censorship*, p. 96)

Here again is the *wholeness* of Lawrence's approach to life, the vital fusion he insists upon between ideals and the living self. Here too is the close tie-in with "the first motive for all human activity" —passionate, purposive action—which certainly involves some form of deep emotional belief which "has the mind's connivance." And as Father Tiverton has observed, this greater motive can only be compared with "the Christian-existentialist theme of 'engagement'." The comparison is a shrewd one, since it indicates a feasible conjunction between Lawrence's work and an existing fund of ideals—and surely the rejuvenation of such ideals would result in far-flung changes for our times. Suppose, for example, that all our churches would found themselves on the "rock" of phallic marriage; or suppose they would at least reemphasize the sacredness of the flesh, the possibility of sexual communion, and the resurrection to organic being. Then they might also serve as founts for the regeneration of the wider body of ideals which constitutes our Western heritage. At least this social and religious vision seems like a valid challenge to our various contemporary faiths—much more valid, in fact, than the religious program in *The Plumed Serpent,* which is the point, in Lawrence's "prophetic" thought, at which most critics stop. But surely Lawrence went beyond that point in his later years, and moved with increasing confidence toward a more relevant vision of social resurrection. In the words of Father Tiverton:

If the Christian 'myth,' as a real operative element in our collective culture, is dead, it is Lawrence who felt this most deeply and agonizingly: and it is he, too, who has seen most clearly that if it is ever to be recovered it will be, not by programmes or research, still less by moral exhortation, but by resurrection. (*D. H. Lawrence and Human Existence,* p. 125)

III

But if social resurrection is our theme, then we must turn at last to the work of art which leads our sympathies in that direction. For the artistic vision gives us concrete rather than abstract knowledge of that theme, as it appeals with dramatic force to the "whole corpus" of our consciousness. Thus *The Man Who Died* is Lawrence's last bequest to his readers, his final vision, and in a poetic sense, the crown of his accomplishment. Granted, the book will trouble the Christian reader at first; but in the light of Father Tiverton's remarks, it must ultimately please him: if the criticism of Christianity is clearly there, if the Christ of Lawrence seems more like a godly prophet than the Son of God, nevertheless He is still the Risen Lord, and the book remains a tribute to His Resurrection, an interpretation which keeps remarkable faith with a central and symbolic meaning of that event, if not with the literal belief:

For God calls even the flesh to the resurrection [writes an early Christian theologian] and promises it eternal life. To announce the good news of salvation to man was in effect to announce it to the flesh. For what is man if not a reasonable being composed of soul and body? Shall we say that the soul in itself is the man? No, it is the soul of the man. And the body alone—is that the man? By no means; we should rather say it is the body of the man. Since, then, neither soul alone nor body alone are man, but the thing called man arises out of their union, when God called man to the resurrection and the life, He called no mere part of man but the whole man, body and soul together in one.[5]

Or as Lawrence poses the same problem:

Church doctrine teaches the resurrection of the body; and if that doesn't mean the whole man, what does it mean? And if man is whole without a woman . . . then I'm damned. (*Letters*, pp. 786-87)

Was Lawrence damned? Not, at any rate, for *The Man Who Died*. But to understand the book at all we must turn, for a moment, to several of his most pertinent objections to modern Christianity.

As early as 1915 Lawrence had begun to criticize

the modern Church for its morbid view of the resurrection story—its emphasis on the tomb, the death,
the wounds, and the cross, above and beyond "the
pale fact of Resurrection." This emphasis left "half of
the year of the soul . . . cold and historiless"; it
meant that the religious drama of life was "ended
at thirty-three"—

But why? Why shall I not rise with my body whole
and perfect, shining with strong life? . . .
The Resurrection is to life, not to death. . . .
Can I not, then, walk this earth in gladness, being
risen from sorrow? Can I not eat with my brother hap-
pily, and with joy kiss my beloved, after my resurrection,
celebrate my marriage in the flesh with feastings, go
about my business eagerly, in the joy of my fellows? Is
heaven impatient for me, and bitter against this earth,
that I should hurry off, or that I should linger pale and
untouched? Is the flesh which was crucified become as
poison to the crowds in the street, or is it as a strong
gladness and hope to them, as the first flower blossom-
ing out of the earth's humus? (*The Rainbow*, pp. 264-65)

Here is *The Man Who Died* in embryonic form,
yet fully endowed with social implications: for "the
crowds in the street," the dramatic scope of Resurrection must include a vision of greater life on earth,
as well as after death. This theme recurs as late as
Apocalypse, where Lawrence holds that the mass of
men have need of a much more powerful source of
inspiration than "pure Christianity"; and in a previ-

ous essay, "The Risen Lord," he makes the Churches answerable to that need:

> The Churches loudly assert: We preach Christ cruci-
> fied!—But in so doing, they preach only half of the Pas-
> sion, and do only half their duty. The Creed says: "Was
> crucified, dead, and buried . . . the third day He rose
> again from the dead." And again, "I believe in the resur-
> rection of the body . . ." So that to preach Christ Cruci-
> fied is to preach half the truth. It is the business of the
> Church to preach Christ born among men—which is
> Christmas; Christ Crucified, which is Good Friday; and
> Christ Risen, which is Easter. And after Easter, till No-
> vember and All Saints, and till Annunciation, the year
> belongs to the Risen Lord: that is, all the full-flowering
> spring, all summer, and the autumn of wheat and fruit,
> all belong to Christ Risen.
>
> But the Churches insist on Christ Crucified, and rob us
> of the blossom and fruit of the year. (*The Later D. H.
> Lawrence*, p. 386)

Given this critical approach, it was inevitable that Lawrence would attempt, at some time, to transform or revitalize the central Christian doctrine of resurrection. In *Lady Chatterley's Lover* he had dealt with "the resurrection of the body" in secular life. Now, in *The Man Who Died*, he applied this theme to the story of the Risen Christ and the Isis-Osiris legend—a combination of "myths" with unmistakable social connotations. But for the moment let us attend to the ritual pattern of the story.

A peasant near Jerusalem acquires a shabby young gamecock, who "by some freak of destiny" grows into a splendid rooster. The rooster hears "the challenge of far-off unseen cocks, in the unknown world," and answers them "with a ringing defiance, never to be daunted." To prevent his escape, a restraining cord has been tied around one of his legs. But the lively cock grows restless under the restraint, and breaks the symbolic cord one morning with a sudden upward leap. Then he flies to the top of the courtyard wall, and crows a triumphant crow—which seems to be the first significant contact of "the man who died" (in spirit rather than flesh) with the raucous voice of life itself:

At the same time, at the same hour before dawn, on the same morning, a man awoke from a long sleep in which he was tied up. He woke numb and cold, inside a carved hole in the rock. Through all the long sleep his body had been full of hurt. He did not open his eyes. Yet he knew that he was awake, and numb, and cold, and rigid, and full of hurt, and tied up. His face was banded with cold bands, his legs were bandaged together. Only his hands were loose. (p. 7)

A few minutes later, as the disillusioned man moves slowly toward the outskirts of the city, the cock crows wildly from a nearby bough, and the sound makes him "shiver as if electricity had touched him." Here again is the electric surge of life, the close connection between man, bird, beast and flower which remains the hallmark of Laurentian fiction. For the ailing stranger now helps the peasant to catch his bird; he takes shelter, for a time, in the man's cottage, and lies in the yard each day, absorbing the sun, healing his wounds, watching the life around him fling itself up "in stormy or subtle wave-crests, foam-tips emerging out of the blue invisible . . . out of the vast invisible sea of strength."

Even the tethered bird is like a "short, sharp wave of life," so that his sexual pounce upon a favorite hen becomes "one wave-tip of life overlapping . . . another"—and to the man who died, "The doom of death was a shadow compared to the raging destiny of life, the determined surge of life." Thus, as the days go by, the young cock becomes dear to him. "'Surely thou art risen to the Father, among birds' [he says]. And the young cock, answering, crowed."

Later the man who died visits the garden near the tomb; he speaks to Madeleine, and begins the critique of his past which runs all through the book: "I too ran to excess," he tells her. "I gave more than I took, and that also is woe and vanity"; later still, he admits his own folly in trying to make life "bubble all alike" when it "bubbles variously"; and he also cites what I take to be the main objection here to Christianity: "I asked them all to serve me with the corpse of their love. And in the end I offered them only the corpse of my love. This is my body—

take and eat—my corpse. . . . I wanted them to love with dead bodies."

These are the chief negations in *The Man Who Died*, but the greater part of the book remains a positive and poetic fable of resurrection. For the Christ-figure now learns to seek the single, quiet way of life, and gradually, as his wounds heal, he achieves his aloneness, and leaves his striving, public self behind him in the tomb. This is the first great step toward resurrection, the step toward isolate selfhood; and inevitably the second step is toward togetherness: to fully achieve "the greater life of the body," the prophet must now discover a woman who will love him, yet leave him his aloneness. So he buys the young cock from the peasant and returns to the world of men as a physician.

On the first night of the outward journey he sleeps at an inn. And again he wakes in the morning to the cock's significant crow: the rooster of the inn is defending his realm from the young challenger; but the young cock kills him and the prophet leaves his bird in command of the local yard: "Thou at least hast found thy kingdom, and the females of thy body. Thy aloneness can take on splendour, polished by the lure of thy hens."

So ends the parable of the cock: the bird has now entered the world of unknown birds, fought his battle, won his kingdom, and established the separateness and togetherness, the aloofness and the commit-

ment, which the man who died must now establish.[6]
Yet the man's "kingdom" is much more difficult to
establish than the bird's. From now on, wherever
he travels, his neighbors try to bully him into com-
pulsive beliefs which threaten his aloneness:

It was the mania of cities and societies and hosts, to lay a
compulsion upon a man, upon all men. For men and
women alike were mad with the egoistic fear of their
own nothingness. And he thought of his own mission,
how he had tried to lay the compulsion of love on all
men. And the old nausea came back on him. For there
was no contact without a subtle attempt to inflict a compulsion. And already he had been compelled even into
death. The nausea of the old wound broke out afresh,
and he looked again on the world with repulsion, dread-
ing its mean contacts. (p. 46)

In January of the same year, however, the prophet
reaches the Syrian coast and meets the virgin priestess of Isis in Search. According to the ancient myth,
the goddess Isis looks for the scattered fragments of
the dead god Osiris, which she must reassemble and
rouse to life, so the god can fecundate her virgin
womb. But Isis is unable to find "the last reality, the
final clue to him, that alone could bring him really
back to her." This clue is the phallus, the living link
between man, woman and life itself, or as Lawrence
calls it elsewhere, "the great old symbol of godly
vitality in a man, and of immediate contact."

Quite obviously the parable of the cock exploits this phallic clue: witness, the book's original title, *The Escaped Cock*. But this is not irreverence on Lawrence's part, nor is it mere *inclusiveness*, or the modern attitude toward sex as "sane" and necessary; instead, the phallus serves here as the *key* to fuller life, and the story bears this meaning out in concrete and dramatic terms. When prophet and priestess first sight each other, for example, they are standing on opposite cliffs, while down below them, on the coast, a slave boy has covered a young slave girl "in the blind, frightened frenzy of a boy's first passion." This furtive, adolescent sexuality is set in contrast with the sacred, healing sexual rite which follows, later on, between the priestess and the man who died. For the young woman takes the stranger for the dead Osiris, and drawn forth by her tenderness, and by his own need to escape from death, he accepts the role and meets her in the mystery of the reborn god. Within the sanctity of her temple, she annoints his wounds with oil, enfolds him in her embrace, and revives him with living warmth; then, as shock after shock of desire runs through him, he returns her embrace and achieves his living wholeness. As he tells us later: "This is the great atonement, the being in touch. The gray sea and the rain, the wet narcissus and the woman I wait for, the invisible Isis and the unseen sun are all in touch, and at one." So he decides to build his life on the "deep-folded, penetrable

rock of the living woman," and their contact is fulfilled as the months draw on.

All this is more than sexuality, *per se:* the "invisible Isis" and the "unseen sun" mean godly vitality,
or the phallic power within man and woman which
Lawrence saw as a force for creative labor; and the
"rock of the living woman" means phallic marriage
itself, or the first element of union in mankind; while
"being in touch" is the soul's transcendence of merely
finite being, its contact with the living God through
life-responsibility, nourishing love, and the wakening of the whole corpus of the human consciousness.
The prophet speaks, in fact, of the "greater day of
the human consciousness," and he "rises to the
Father" (to godly vitality) through this complex
combination of change and achievement.

Nor does Lawrence try to divorce him from his
historic association with the Christian Church. The
wedding of pagan and Christian legends into a single fable seems to bear this out, and the impregnation of the priestess tends to confirm it: for the
prophet, forced to flee for his life, assures her firmly
of his inevitable return; and his final words are
packed with social implication:

I have sowed the seed of my life and my resurrection,
and put my touch forever upon the choice woman of this
day, and I carry her perfume in my flesh like essence of
roses. She is dear to me in the middle of my being. But

the gold and flowing serpent is coiling up again, to sleep at the root of my tree.

So let the boat carry me. Tomorrow is another day.

The meaning of this passage seems clear: through the prophet's resurrection comes social regeneration, since the "seed" of his life is the pagan-Christian child of the future, and "the gold and flowing serpent" means power, in the man himself, for further creative activity—while "day" can only be understood, in Laurentian terms, as the time for collective, purposive labor—for the resurrection, perhaps, of the Christian Church itself. At any rate, it is precisely this social aspect of the resurrection which Lawrence stresses in a companion essay, called "The Risen Lord":

If Jesus rose a full man in the flesh, He rose to do his share in the world's work, something he really liked doing. . . . If Jesus rose a full man in the flesh, He rose to continue His fight with the hard-boiled conventionalists like Roman judges and Jewish priests and moneymakers of every sort. But this time, it would no longer be the fight of self-sacrifice that would end in crucifixion. This time it would be a freed man fighting to shelter the rose of life from being trampled on by the pigs. This time, if Satan attempted temptation in the wilderness, the Risen Lord would answer: Satan . . . The earth is the Lord's and the fullness thereof, and I, the Risen Lord, am here to take possession. . . . What are riches, and glory, and honour, and might, and power, to me who have died and lost my self-importance? That's why I am going to take them all from you, Mammon, because I care nothing about them. I am going to destroy all your values, Mammon; all your money values and conceit values, I am going to destroy them all.

Because only life is lovely, and you, Mammon, prevent life. . . . I love the movement of life, and the beauty of life, O Mammon, since I am risen, I love the beauty of life intensely; columbine flowers, for example, the way they dangle, or the delicate way a young girl sits and wonders, or the rage with which a man turns and kicks a fool dog that suddenly attacks him—beautiful that, the swift fierce turn and lunge of a kick, then the quivering pause for the next attack; or even the slightly silly glow that comes over some men as they are getting tipsy—it still is a glow, beautiful; or the swift look a woman fetches me, when she would really like me to go off with her, but she is troubled; or the real compassion I saw a woman express for a man who slipped and wrenched his foot: life, the beauty, the beauty of life! But that which is anti-life, Mammon, like you, and money, and machines and prostitution, and all that tangled mass of self-importance and greediness and self-conscious conceit which adds up to Mammon, I hate it. I hate it, Mammon, I hate you and am going to push you off the face of the earth, Mammon, you great mob-thing, fatal to men. (*The Later D. H. Lawrence,* pp. 391-93)

So the Risen Christ is Lord of Life, and the Church which preaches Him must be reborn as the Church of Life: that is the trend of *The Man Who*

Died, and its point of connection, as well, with *Lady Chatterley's Lover;* for the latter book marks out the rites of phallic marriage, while the former links those rites with the larger pattern of Western civilization; and the two books, taken together, give us a coherent, vital and dramatic vision of human existence—a religion of life, a fund of rejuvenated ideals, a creative pattern for the future. And there is the final vision of a major English novelist—even the final measure of his greatness, if we can take our cue from Stephen Spender's poem, "I Think Continually of Those Who Were Truly Great": [7]

Near the snow, near the sun, in the highest fields,
See how these names are fêted by the waving grass
And by the streamers of white cloud
And whispers of wind in the listening sky.
The names of those who in their lives fought for life,
Who wore at their hearts the fire's centre.
Born of the sun, they travelled a short while toward the sun,
And left the vivid air signed with their honour.

Surely D. H. Lawrence ranks first among those who "fought for life" in his own generation of writers; and surely he waged this fight with greatest success in his major and minor novels—and waged it, first and foremost, as a creative and prophetic artist; for with Lawrence, the two terms are inseparable.

NOTES

1. In the first draft of the novel, the gamekeeper is actually the secretary for a local Communist league, and is therefore actively engaged in a collective, purposive movement; but Connie seems to voice the author's usual doubts about Communism (as "atavistic materialism"), and the novel ends on an uncertain note. By the third and last version, the belief is dropped with respect to Mellors, and the parlor intellectuals rip it apart in an early chapter. Nevertheless, the original use of the theme reveals how deeply Lawrence was concerned with the problem of man's worldly work, to the point where he would even experiment with a notion he had already cast aside in *Kangaroo*.

2. Since Lawrence presents a realistic (and not a metaphorical) program in *The Plumed Serpent*, the book is subject to realistic appraisal. Even so, the ritual sacrifice of two enemy brigands and the desecration of a church are not the same as planned mass slaughters. It seems significant, moreover, that General Cipriano scorns modern methods of warfare in the novel, in favor of sudden night raids by his guerrilla bands: always Lawrence is most romantic when he tries to be fiercely realistic. His real failure, then, remains the omission of effective checks against evil within the newly established state; the *coup d'etat* itself is relatively bloodless.

3. All of Lawrence's utopian states are static and paradisal (see "Autobiographical Fragment," in this respect, in *Phoenix*). His concept of the "spirit of place," and of the magnetic pull of the earth's center, led him to conceive of the world in terms of local and remarkably quiescent religious states, governed peacefully by superior prophets. Of course,

this meant a complete rejection of international flux and mechanized industry, and a return to religious towns and agrarian economies—hence the appeal which the Etruscan civilization held for him in *Etruscan Places*. Though he admitted himself that spontaneous action was an extraordinarily difficult achievement, he obviously tried to construct a purely spontaneous form of society, something like the Confucian system of internal, interpersonal, and (finally) universal equilibrium. Indeed, his use of rites and ceremonies is very like the Confucian concept of Music, or the ritualistic ordering of the emotions, as an aid to universal equilibrium.

4. Lawrence preached a cosmic and vital God, in whose vitality human beings could partake *in time*. But the Christian God remains largely outside the universe, and the contact established with Him is usually spiritual, static, and timeless; it occurs, that is, during the timeless moment of prayer, and even Lawrence gives credence to this experience: witness the cathedral scene in *The Rainbow*, where Will Brangwen's soul achieves consummation with the Christian infinite. But his wife Anna shows him that his religion seems to exclude a great part of life, and this remains the author's steadfast view: that "pure Christianity" is valid for a few individuals and for part of man's nature, but it cannot satisfy a whole society and it also fails to appeal to the impersonal or collective side of human nature:

> The religions of renunciation, meditation, self-knowledge, pure morality are for individuals, and even then, not for complete individuals. But they express the individual side of man's nature. They isolate this side of his nature. And they cut off the other side of his nature, the collective side. . . . Of the positive side of Christianity, the peace of meditation and the joy of unselfish service, the rest from ambition and the pleasure of knowledge, we find nothing

in the Apocalypse. Because the Apocalypse is for the non-individual side of a man's nature, written from the thwarted collective self, whereas meditation and unselfish service are for pure individuals, isolate. Pure Christianity anyhow *cannot* fit a nation, or society at large. The great war made it obvious. It can only fit individuals. The collective whole must have some other inspiration. (*Apocalypse,* pp. 23, 24)

As I have already pointed out, Lawrence finds the source of such inspiration in sexual consummation, on the one hand, and in "passionate, purposive activity," on the other. He seems to share this latter concept with Goethe, Carlyle, and Ruskin, though it is also Calvinistic in origin.

5. This quotation appears in Etienne Gilson's *The Spirit of Mediaeval Philosophy* (p. 171), as Gilson attempts to distinguish between the current stress on the soul's immortality and the belief of early theologians in the unity of man. For example:

One of the surprises in store for the historian of Christian thought lies in its insistence on the value, dignity and perpetuity of the human body. . . . St. Bonaventure, St. Thomas Aquinas, Duns Scotus, I will even say St. Francis of Assisi himself—one and all were men who looked benignly on matter, respected their bodies, extolled its dignity, and would never have wished a separate destiny for body and soul. (pp. 168-69)

6. This pattern seems to follow that of *The Rainbow,* where dramatic emphasis is placed upon the thrust outward from the Brangwen farm to the unknown world of men. In other words, the parable includes both aspects of the love-labor scheme, as does the prophet's future experience.

7. *Poems by Stephen Spender,* pp. 45-46. Spender probably had Lawrence (among others) in mind when he wrote this poem. At least the thought and imagery seem quite

Laurentian, both in the verse already quoted and in the one which precedes it:

What is precious, is never to forget
The essential delight of the blood drawn from ageless
   springs
Breaking through rocks in worlds before our earth.
Never to deny its pleasure in the morning simple light
Nor its grave evening demand for love.
Never to allow gradually the traffic to smother
With noise and fog, the flowering of the Spirit.

WORKS CITED

Aldington, Richard. *D. H. Lawrence: Portrait of a Genius But. . . .* New York, 1950.

Amon, Frank. "D. H. Lawrence and the Short Story." *The Achievement of D. H. Lawrence,* ed. Frederick J. Hoffman and Harry T. Moore. Norman (Oklahoma), 1953.

Balzac, Honore de. *Old Goriot.* Harmondsworth (England), 1951.

Beach, Joseph Warren. "Impressionism: Lawrence." *The Twentieth Century Novel: Studies in Technique.* New York, 1932.

Betsky, Seymour. "Rhythm and Theme: D. H. Lawrence's *Sons and Lovers.*" *The Achievement of D. H. Lawrence,* ed. Frederick J. Hoffman and Harry T. Moore. Norman (Oklahoma), 1953.

Butler, Samuel. *The Way of All Flesh.* Modern Library, New York, 193——.

Cassirer, Ernst. *An Essay on Man.* New Haven, 1944.

———. *Language and Myth,* New York, 1946.

Chambers, Jessie [E. T.]. *D. H. Lawrence: A Personal Record.* London, 1935.

Dickens, Charles. *Hard Times.* London, 1951.

Fergusson, Francis. "D. H. Lawrence's Sensibility." *Forms of Modern Fiction,* ed. William Van O'Connor. Minneapolis, 1948.

Gide, André. *Dostoievsky*. Norfolk (Connecticut), 1949.

Gilson, Etienne. *The Spirit of Mediæval Philosophy*. New York, 1940.

Greene, Thomas. "Lawrence and the Quixotic Hero." *Sewanee Review*, LIX (1951), 559-73.

Gregory, Horace. *Pilgrim of the Apocalypse: A Critical Study of D. H. Lawrence*. New York, 1933.

Hoffman, Frederick J., and Harry T. Moore, ed. *The Achievement of D. H. Lawrence*. Norman (Oklahoma), 1953.

——. *Freudianism and the Literary Mind*. Baton Rouge, 1945.

Lawrence, D. H. *Aaron's Rod*. New York, 1922.

——. *Apocalypse*. New York, 1932.

——. "A Propos of Lady Chatterley's Lover," in *Sex, Literature and Censorship*.

——, and M. L. Skinner. *The Boy in the Bush*. New York, 1924.

——. *Fantasia of the Unconscious*. New York, 1922.

——. *The First Lady Chatterley*. New York, 1944.

——. *Kangaroo*. New York, 1923.

——. *Lady Chatterley's Lover*. Florence, 1928.

——. *The Later D. H. Lawrence*, ed. William York Tindall. New York, 1952.

——. *The Letters of D. H. Lawrence*, ed. Aldous Huxley. New York, 1932.

——. *The Lost Girl*. New York, 1921.

——. *The Lovely Lady*. New York, 1946.

——. *The Man Who Died*. New York, 1928.

——. *Phoenix: The Posthumous Papers of D. H. Lawrence*. New York, 1936.

——. *The Plumed Serpent*. New York, 1926.

——. *The Portable D. H. Lawrence*, ed. Diana Trilling. New York, 1950.

———. *Psychoanalysis and the Unconscious*. New York, 1921.

———. *The Rainbow*. Modern Library, New York, 1927.

———. *Reflections on the Death of a Porcupine*. Philadelphia, 1925.

———. *Sea and Sardinia*. New York, 1921.

———. *Sex, Literature and Censorship*, ed. Harry T. Moore. New York, 1953.

———. *Sons and Lovers*. Modern Library, New York, 1923.

———. *Studies in Classic American Literature*. New York, 1923.

———. *The Trespasser*. London, 1950.

———. *Twilight in Italy*. New York, 1916.

———. *The White Peacock*. London, 1949.

———. *Women in Love*. Modern Library, New York, 1937.

Leavis, F. R. *The Great Tradition*. New York, 1948.

———. "The Novel as Dramatic Poem: 'St. Mawr.'" *Scrutiny*, XVII (1950), 38-52.

———. "The Novel as Dramatic Poem: 'Women in Love.'" *Scrutiny*, XVII (1950-51), 203-20, 318-30; XVIII (1951), 18-31.

———. "The Novel as Dramatic Poem: 'The Rainbow.'" *Scrutiny*, XVIII (1951-52), 197-210, 273-87; XIX (1952), 15-30.

Meredith, George. *Diana of the Crossways*. New York, 1931.

Moore, Harry T., and Frederick J. Hoffman, ed. *The Achievement of D. H. Lawrence*. Norman (Oklahoma), 1953.

———. *The Life and Works of D. H. Lawrence*. New York, 1951.

———, ed. *Sex, Literature and Censorship*. New York, 1953.

O'Connor, William Van, ed. *Forms of Modern Fiction*. Minneapolis, 1948.

Ruskin, John. *The Stones of Venice*. New York, 1895. Vol. II.

Schorer, Mark. "Fiction With a Great Burden." *Kenyon Review*, XIV (1952), 162-68.

————. "Technique as Discovery." *Forms of Modern Fiction,* ed. William Van O'Connor. Minneapolis, 1948.

Spender, Stephen. *Poems by Stephen Spender.* New York, 1934.

Taine, Hippolyte A. *History of English Literature.* London, 1880. Vol. IV.

Tindall, William York, ed. *The Later D. H. Lawrence.* New York, 1952.

Tiverton, Father William [William Robert Jarrett-Kerr]. *D. H. Lawrence and Human Existence.* New York, 1951.

Trilling, Diana, ed. *The Portable D. H. Lawrence.* New York, 1950.

Valéry, Paul. *Selected Writings.* New York, 1950.

Van Ghent, Dorothy. *The English Novel: Form and Function.* New York, 1953.

Vivas, Eliseo. "Lawrence's Problems." *Kenyon Review,* III (1941), 83-94.

Wildi, Max. "The Birth of Expressionism in the Work of D. H. Lawrence." *English Studies,* XIX (1937), 241-59.

INDEX